VINTAGE STYLE
QUILTS

VINTAGE-STYLE QUILTS

25 STEP-BY-STEP PATCHWORK AND QUILTING PROJECTS USING NEW AND OLD MATERIALS

Flora Roberts

Photography by Gloria Nicol

CREATIVE HOMEOWNER®, Upper Saddle River, New Jersey

To Anne Roberts

First published in the US in 2004 by

CRE▲TIVE
ARTS & CRAFTS™

An imprint of Creative Homeowner®,
Upper Saddle River, NJ

Creative Homeowner® is a registered trademark of
Federal Marketing

First published in 2004 by Cico Books Ltd
32 Great Sutton Street, London EC1V 0NB
Copyright © Cico Books 2004

Current printing (last digit) 10 9 8 7 6 5 4 3 2 1

Library of Congress card number: 2003111561

ISBN 1–58011–172–6

Illustrations by Kate Simunek
Edited by Sarah Hoggett
Photography by Gloria Nicol
Designed by Janet James

CREATIVE HOMEOWNER
A Division of Federal Marketing Corp.
24 Park Way
Upper Saddle River, NJ 07458

www.creativehomeowner.com

Printed and bound in Singapore

Contents

Introduction

I've been interested in textiles and sewing for almost as long as I can remember, and vintage fabrics have always fascinated me. Their faded patterns and colors speak to me of a bygone age when life was lived at a slower and more gentle pace than today. Over the years, I've amassed a treasure trove of fabrics from different eras—crisp Victorian linen sheets and lace-trimmed handkerchiefs; 1930s' dresses in soft shades of pink and eau-de-Nil green; delicate antique silks decorated with the most exquisite embroidery. They are far too beautiful to be consigned to a closet, never again to see the light of day, but sadly some of them were so badly worn in places that repairing them was not an option. That is when I decided to see if I could incorporate them into my own textile work in some way, to rejuvenate them and give them a new lease on life in the 21st century—and patchwork, which enabled me to salvage scraps from a larger piece, was the obvious solution.

Using vintage fabrics

Patchwork means that you can make an expensive vintage fabric such as silk go much further, by combining it with other fabrics. It's amazing how even a tiny amount of a vintage fabric can be enough to transform a piece made mainly from modern textiles into something with a period feel. At the same time, the combination of vintage and modern allows you to blend such items into the contemporary home with ease. Reusing scraps is a long-established tradition in patchwork and quilting; indeed, patchwork really came into its own in the 19th century as an economical way of recycling material. As the best museum pieces show, using scraps does not necessarily mean that the end result looks as if the maker was simply making do with what she had at hand.

Choosing vintage fabrics

Color is instrumental in your choice of fabric. I start every project by gathering together fabrics that I think might be useful—vintage garments and household linen that I have collected over the years, unused fabric or small off-cuts from clothes or furnishings that I have made—and sorting them into groups of colors that go well together. Fabrics that look a little dull or uninteresting on their own can change their character completely when they are combined with other textiles. Get the overall color combinations right, and you can happily mix floral prints with candy-colored stripes or snippets of embroidery with bold, solid colors. Balance the patterned and colored fabrics with neutral whites and creams, and you have a cool and contemporary style that looks good in any setting.

The other wonderful thing about using vintage fabrics in your home furnishings is that it gives you the opportunity to make things that are quite unique: the chances of anyone else being able to find exactly the same fabrics as you are slim, and there's certainly no risk of walking into your local department store and coming across dozens of quilts or cushion covers that are identical to the one you've just made!

This book is intended to provide you with inspiration for reusing vintage fabrics to create new pieces for a contemporary home and lifestyle. You will no doubt have your own favorite color combinations and styles; you may even have pieces with their own special memories or associations, such as a favorite dress or a scrap of lace from your grandmother's much-loved shawl. I hope that this book will, at the very least, open your eyes to the potential of mixing the old with the new.

Where to buy vintage fabrics

Unfortunately, large quantities of vintage fabric are hard to come by: being part of history, they are a finite resource. However, because there has been a recent resurgence of interest in them, you can find good examples in antique shops and some markets. Yard sales and thrift stores are other good sources; you can often pick up interesting and unusual fabrics very cheaply.

In my experience, the most commonly available and least expensive vintage fabrics are linens used for domestic purposes, such as old sheets or tablecloths. These sometimes have wonderful examples of embroidery on them and, as they are made from natural fibers, they can be dyed in a range of fantastic colors and are therefore extremely versatile.

Vintage prints are less easy to come by. I go to many antique textile fairs to find them. Enquire at your local antique shop: it is likely that the shop assistant will know the dates and venues for events in your area.

Caring for vintage fabrics

If you can face buying fabrics that are in a less than perfect condition, do not underestimate the rejuvenating power of simple soap flakes that you can buy from most general stores. As one antiques dealer told me, soap flakes can lift even tea stains—so you have to be careful that you don't fade an original print as well.

I recommend that you carefully hand-wash all fabrics before using them. Even new cottons can sometimes shrink a bit, and prewashing prevents problems arising later when you steam iron patchwork pieces to make them beautifully flat.

You should also test all the fabrics that you are planning to use to make sure that they are colorfast. To do this, place a few drops of water on a small section and then dab the fabric with blotting paper to see whether any color comes off.

When the time comes to launder any of the projects in this book, always hand-wash them. Some of my projects involve hand stitching and this tends to make them more fragile than machine-stitched objects.

CHAPTER 1

CUSHIONS AND COVERS

Log-Cabin Cushion

Star Cushion and Matching Bolster

Yo-yo Floor Cushion

Kimono Cushions

Tie-on Quilted Cushion

Log-Cabin Cushion

A traditional 19th-century pattern, this type of patchwork takes its name from the log cabins of the homestead pioneers. There are many variations on the basic pattern, but they all consist of stitching strips of fabric around a center square, with each successive strip being slightly longer than the preceding one. Traditionally, all the strips are the same width and the center square is twice the width of the strips.

Many Log Cabin patterns rely on the contrast between light and dark fabrics for their effect; often, a secondary pattern emerges when several identical blocks are joined together. In this project, each block is slightly different, which gives you the perfect opportunity to use up tiny scraps of fabric from your stash of thrift-store and market finds.

Left: With its carefully selected colors, patterns, and textures, this fresh-looking cushion would look good in any setting—town or country, vintage chic or contemporary cool.

Log-Cabin Cushion

You will need

- Nine 6-inch muslin or cotton foundation squares
- Scraps of cotton fabric or ribbon in colors of your choice
- 16-inch square of thin cotton to back the patchwork
- Enough corded piping to go around the edge of the cushion
- Two 16 x 10½-inch pieces of linen
- Matching sewing thread
- Two large buttons
- 15-inch square cushion pad

1. To work out the position of the first piece of fabric, draw diagonal lines from corner to corner across the foundation square, taking care not to stretch the fabric. Place the center square right side up in the middle of the foundation square, aligning the corners with the drawn diagonal lines.

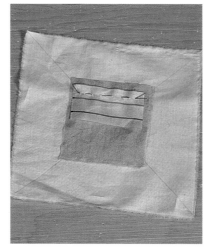

2. Place the first strip (which should be the length of one side and half the width of the center square) on top of the center square, right sides together, and baste it in place. (It is best to cut each strip slightly longer than you need and trim it once you have stitched it in place if necessary.)

3. Machine-stitch the strip to the center square, fold the strip back to the right side, and press with your fingertips or a warm iron so that the strip lies flat.

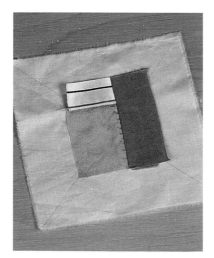

4. Add the next strip, which should be the length of the center square plus the width of the first strip, in the same way.

5. Add two more strips to complete the square, increasing the length of each strip as you go.

6. Here, three more "rounds" of four strips each have been added to fill up the foundation square.

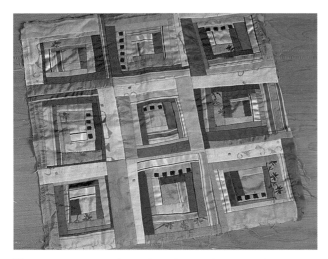

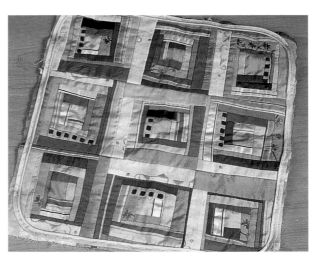

7. Make nine blocks in total, and stitch them together in three rows of three, taking ½-inch seams. Press the seams to one side. Sew the completed patchwork top to a piece of backing fabric—thin cotton or muslin is ideal.

8. Following the instructions on page 124, make enough corded piping to go all around the top of the cushion. With the patchwork top right side up, stitch the piping to the top of the cushion with the raw edges facing outward.

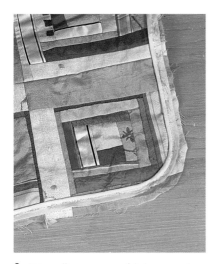

9. Trim off any excess fabric around the corners, making sure you don't cut into the piping. Trimming makes the corners of the cushion cover less bulky so that the cushion pad will fit more neatly inside.

10. Cut two pieces of linen for the back of the cushion, allowing 2 inches of overlap on each piece. Make a ½-inch seam along the overlap edge of each piece. Make two buttonholes on the overlap edge of one piece, 1 inch from the edge. (See page 126.)

11. With the buttonholed piece on top and the seam of each piece underneath, baste the overlapped edges of the two back pieces of the cushion together. This prevents them from slipping out of position when you machine-stitch the base to the top.

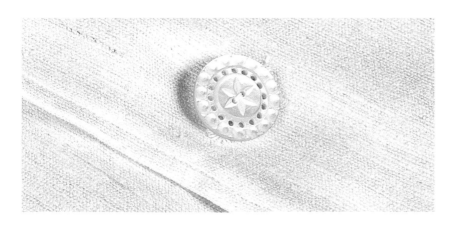

12. Right sides together, stitch the back pieces to the patchwork top, following the stitched line of the piping as closely as possible. Turn the cushion cover right side out, and stitch on the buttons to finish.

Star Cushion and Matching Bolster

One of the beauties of patchwork is that, even if parts of a fabric are badly worn or torn, you can still use the parts that are in good condition and give the piece a new lease on life. This cushion and matching bolster incorporate a rich turquoise silk from a damaged antique kimono. I have tried to give them the same feeling of sophistication that I think the kimono would once have had.

For the cushion, which features a patchwork star motif, I juxtaposed the turquoise kimono fabric with raw silk in a similar color. For the bolster, I combined a strip of the kimono fabric with some antique French lace and linen. Both the cushion and the bolster are trimmed with dark pink piping, which accentuates the delicate flowers of the kimono silk.

Left: Both contemporary-looking and timeless, this elegant cushion and bolster combine the slightly rough texture of white linen with the smooth, jewel-like sheen of embroidered silk.

Star Cushion

You will need

- APPROX. 30 x 9 INCHES PATTERNED KIMONO FABRIC
- APPROX. 30 x 9 INCHES RAW SILK IN A SIMILAR COLOR
- 16-INCH SQUARE THIN COTTON TO BACK THE PATCHWORK (OPTIONAL)
- 24-INCH SQUARE WHITE LINEN FOR THE CUSHION BACK
- 50 x 3½-INCH STRIP WHITE LINEN FOR THE SIDE PANEL
- 50 INCHES CORDED PIPING
- THREE BUTTONS
- MATCHING SEWING THREADS
- READY-MADE CUSHION PAD, 15 INCHES IN DIAMETER AND 2½ INCHES DEEP

1. Using the templates on page 110, cut out six diamond-shaped backing papers for the central star and six curved-edge segments to go around the edges. Cut out three patterned and three solid-colored fabric patches from each shape, adding ½ inch all around each piece. Baste each patch to a backing paper. Right sides together, overstitch the edges of the diamonds to form the central star, alternating patterned and solid-colored fabrics.

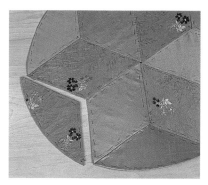

2. Right sides together, carefully overstitch the curved-edge segments that you prepared in Step 1 around the edge of the star, again alternating patterned and solid-colored fabrics. The circular patchwork top of the cushion is now complete.

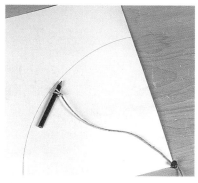

4. Fold a large piece of paper in four, tie a length of string around a pencil, measure the radius of the cushion top plus 1 inch, and pin the string to the center fold in the paper. Draw a quarter-circle; then unfold the paper and cut out the whole circle.

5. Cut the pattern in two to make two unevenly sized pieces. Pin to the linen base fabric, adding 3 inches along each straight edge, and cut out. Hem each straight edge. Stitch three buttonholes along the straight edge of the smaller piece. (See page 126.)

6. Baste the smaller base piece on top of the larger one, overlapping them by about 2½ inches and making sure that the seams are on the underside. (Place the patchworked top over the base to check that they are the same size, and adjust if necessary.)

8. Right sides together, baste the side panel to the top, easing the fabric around the curve. Machine-stitch, following the stitching on the piping.

9. Attach the base of the cushion to the side panel in the same way, and seam it at the side so that it runs continuously around the cushion edge.

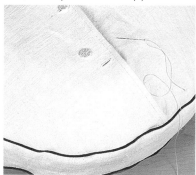

10. Turn the cushion cover right side out, and sew decorative buttons onto the base of the cushion to complete. Insert the cushion pad.

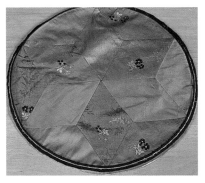

3. Remove the backing papers. If you are using very flimsy, lightweight fabric for the pieced top, back it with thin cotton. Following the instructions on page 124, make enough corded piping to go all around the top and the base of the cushion. With the pieced cushion top right side up, stitch the piping to the top of the cushion with the raw edges facing outward.

7. With the base piece right side up, stitch corded piping around the outer edge ½ inch from the edge, with the raw edge facing outward.

Bolster

You will need

- 23 x 2½ inches pink silk
- 23 x 2½ inches lace
- 23 x 7 inches kimono silk
- 23 x 8½ inches white linen to back the kimono silk and lace
- 23 x 11½ inches white linen
- 16 x 8 inches white linen for bolster ends
- Enough corded piping to go around the ends of the bolster
- 8-inch zipper
- Ready-made bolster pad, 18 inches long x 7 inches in diameter

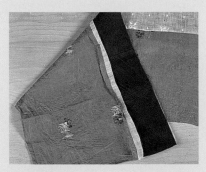

1. Place the lace on top of the pink silk. Right sides together, stitch the silk-backed lace to the kimono silk, taking a ½-inch seam. Press the seam open.

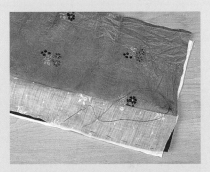

2. Baste the white linen backing piece to the back of the silk and lace piece made in Step 1. (The silk is very delicate; backing it makes it stronger.) Machine-stitch the pieces together.

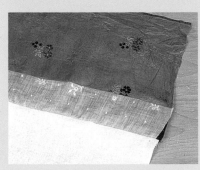

3. Taking a ½-inch seam, stitch one long edge of the remaining rectangle of white linen to the raw long edge of the lace. Press the seam open.

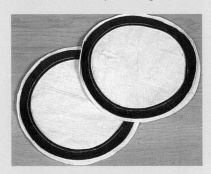

4. Make corded piping to go around the bolster ends. (See page 124.) Right sides facing upward and the raw edges of the piping facing outward, stitch on the piping ½ inch from the edge.

5. Right sides together, pin or baste the long pieced strip to the end pieces and machine stitch in place.

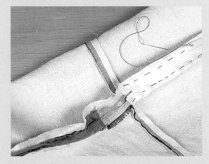

6. Fold over the excess fabric, and make a seam, leaving an opening for the zipper. Insert the zipper. (See page 125.)

Yo-yo Floor Cushion

This is an inexpensive and simple way of accessorizing a plain cushion. The yo-yo patchwork technique shown here is an age-old method used to make lace-like structures; sometimes they are very small in scale, with padding inserted into each disk to make them more sturdy. I made the yo-yos from vintage silks used in lingerie and patterned scarves.

This project uses a ready-made floor cushion, 26 inches square—although you could, of course, make your own. If your cushion is a different size, divide the width of the cushion by ten to find the size of each finished yo-yo, and then double this measurement and add $1/2$ inch to give you the diameter of each ungathered circle of silk.

You will need

- READY-MADE FLOOR CUSHION, 26 INCHES SQUARE
- ONE HUNDRED $5^{1}/_{2}$-INCH CIRCLES OF SILK IN ASSORTED COLORS AND PATTERNS
- MATCHING SEWING THREAD

Left: The pinks and reds of the silk yo-yos make a dramatic statement against the white cover of this large floor cushion.

1. Fold over the edges of each silk circle by about 1/4 inch. Knot a length of thread, and work a single row of running stitches around the folded edge.

2. Gently pull up the thread to gather the yo-yo. Secure the end of the thread with a couple of backstitches or a knot, and cut off any excess thread.

3. Arrange each yo-yo so that the gathered stitches are in the center. Place a damp cloth over the top, and gently press with an iron. Join the yo-yos together with a few tiny whipstitches. Make ten rows of ten yo-yos each, and then join the rows together in the same way.

4. Position the yo-yos on the cushion cover. Attach the yo-yos on the outer rows to the cushion cover with a few tiny whipstitches.

Kimono Cushions

These two cushions are not only very decorative objects, but they also make good head rests. Both cushions incorporate embroidered silk from a kimono. The embroidery is so delicate that I wanted to use a rough, woven linen as a contrast. I also used the silk lining of the kimono as part of the square patchwork for one of the cushions and for the ends on the other cushion. It is nice to make use of a fabric that doesn't normally see the light of day.

The measurements given here are for a cushion pad measuring 10 x 5 inches. If your cushion pad has the same proportions but a different size, work out the size of the squares on the patchwork cushion by measuring the length and width of one side, halving the length to find the finished size of each square patch and then adding $^1/_2$ inch all around each patch. For the end pieces, work out the finished size and add $^1/_2$-inch all around.

Above: The Linen and Silk-Strip Cushion is the perfect way to use up a long, thin strip of a precious fabric.

Right: The Square-Patterned Cushion exploits the effect of complementary colors (an orangey terracotta and blue) and cleverly juxtaposes small pieces of embroidered silk with solid colors.

Square-Patterned Kimono Cushion

You will need

- Four 6-inch squares of embroidered kimono silk
- Four 6-inch squares of solid-colored silk in a contrasting color
- Two 6-inch squares of white linen for end pieces
- 21 x 11 inches lining fabric
- Enough corded piping to go around the two end pieces
- 8-inch zipper
- Matching sewing thread

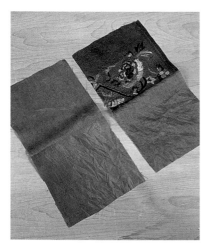

1. Alternating embroidered and solid-colored silks, stitch together the squares, taking a 1/2-inch seam allowance. Using a warm iron, press the seams open.

2. Continue assembling the patchwork until you have four rows of two squares each. Press the seams open with a warm iron so that the patchworked piece lies flat.

3. Baste the lining fabric to the patchwork piece. (The silk that I chose for the cushion was very delicate and worn, and the lining gives it strength and weight.)

4. Following the instructions on page 124, make enough corded piping to go all around the two end pieces. With the right side of the end piece facing upward and the raw edges of the piping facing outward, stitch on the piping.

5. Right sides together, carefully baste and then machine-stitch the end pieces to the patchwork piece, stitching as close to the stitching line of the piping as possible.

6. Trim away the excess fabric, pin the zipper in place, and stitch the back seam and the zipper in place. (See page 125.) Turn the cushion right side out, and insert the cushion pad.

Linen and Silk-Strip Kimono Cushion

You will need

- 21 x 6½ inches white linen
- 21 x 3½ inches white linen
- 21 x 3 inches kimono silk
- 21 x 3 inches white linen to back the silk

- Two 6-inch squares of white linen for end pieces
- Enough corded piping to go around the two end pieces
- 8-inch zipper
- Matching sewing thread

Stitch the fabrics together, taking ½-inch seams and sandwiching the kimono silk and its linen backing between the other two pieces of linen. Cut two 6-inch squares of white linen for the end pieces, and then make up the cushion cover following Steps 4 to 6 of the Square-Patterned Cushion, opposite.

Tie-on Quilted Cushion

This tie-on cushion for a garden or kitchen chair incorporates a decorative embroidered design that is worked in a simple running stitch, using several strands of embroidery floss to hold the layers of fabric together

A floral design forms the center of the quilting pattern, with random stitching over the rest of the cushion—a simple but effective way of making even the plainest of fabrics look like something quite out of the ordinary. You need to consider the colors of the stitches carefully, as they affect the overall appearance of the chair cover. However, part of the charm of this design is its informality, so don't worry about making your stitches too precise and even.

The fabric quantities given on the next page are for a chair seat that is approximately 13 inches square. You may need to adjust them to fit your own chair; instructions for making a pattern are given on page 126.

Left: Pink and blue—a summery-looking color combination for a simple garden chair. The quilting stitches add a much-needed contrast of texture.

Tie-on Quilted Cushion

You will need

- TRACING PAPER OR THIN PAPER
- 14-INCH SQUARE THIN COTTON FOR CHAIR-COVER TOP
- 14-INCH SQUARE LIGHTWEIGHT BATTING
- 14-INCH SQUARE COTTON TO BACK THE QUILTED CHAIR-COVER TOP
- 14-INCH SQUARE ROUGH LINEN TO BACK THE CUSHION

- ENOUGH CORDED PIPING TO GO AROUND THE EDGE OF THE CUSHION
- FOUR 12 x 1½-INCH PIECES LINEN FOR TIES
- APPROX. 3 YARDS READY-MADE BIAS BINDING
- MATCHING SEWING THREAD
- QUILTING OR EMBROIDERY HOOP

- QUILTING NEEDLE
- EMBROIDERY FLOSS IN COLORS OF YOUR CHOICE
- PAPER TO MAKE A PATTERN
- CHALK POWDER

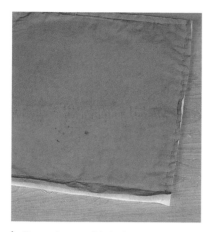

1. Baste the top fabric, batting, and backing for the quilted cushion together.

2. Trace the pattern on page 111 (or any other decorative pattern of your choice) onto paper. Using a sharp needle, prick large holes along the lines of the design.

3. Pin the paper to the fabric you are using for the quilted top. Push chalk powder through the holes to transfer the pattern to the fabric. Alternatively, use a fadeaway pen (available from good needlecraft and quilt supply stores).

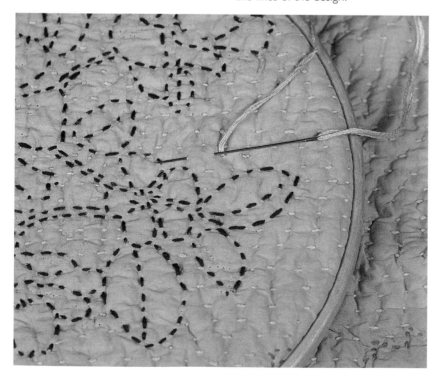

4. Place the fabric in a quilting or embroidery hoop. Using a quilting needle and embroidery floss in colors of your choice, quilt the lines of the design by hand using tiny running stitches. I used a burgundy red for the flower, yellow for the flower center, and lilac and orange for the background. Work running stitches randomly over the rest of the cushion to hold the layers together.

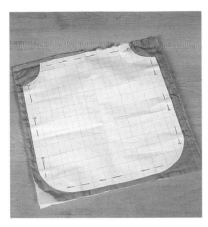

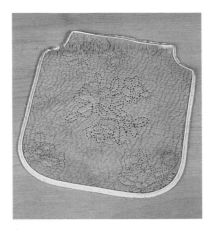

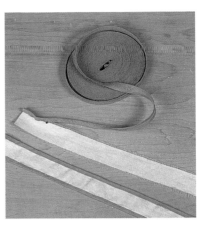

5. Make a paper pattern the size of your chair seat. (See page 126.) Pin the pattern to the quilted top, and cut it out. (Don't worry if you cut through some of the quilting stitches, as the edges will be covered.)

6. Following the instructions on page 124, make enough corded piping to go around the edge of the chair cover. Machine-stitch it to the top of the cover, with the raw edges of the piping facing outward.

7. Take ready-made bias binding in a color that matches the main fabric of the cushion top, fold it around the edges of the linen ties, and slipstitch it in place.

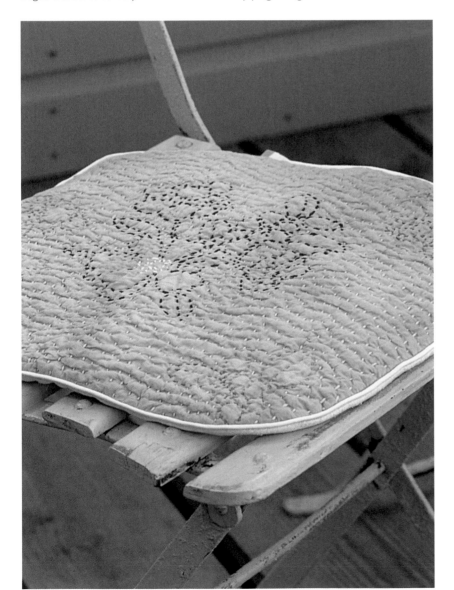

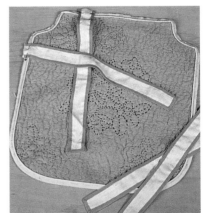

8. Pin the ties to the top and sides of the quilted cover.

9. Right sides together, baste the linen backing fabric to the quilted cover. Machine-stitch around the edge, leaving a gap of about 4 inches for turning. Turn the cover right side out, and slipstitch the gap closed.

CHAPTER 2

HOUSEHOLD LINEN

Broderie Anglaise Lavender Bags

Laundry Bag

Clothespin Bag

Vintage-Ribbon Pincushion

Padded Coat Hanger with Heart-Shaped Lavender Bag

Basket Liner

Table Runner, Place Mat, and Napkin Ring

Linen Tablecloth with Patchwork Border

Hot-Water-Bottle Cover

Broderie-Anglaise Lavender Bags

In Victorian times, broderie anglaise was widely used to decorate household linen, and it is therefore very easy to find in antiques markets and thrift stores. For these pretty little lavender bags, I dyed it in delicate pastel shades to tone in with the other fabrics. I then backed it with either a solid-colored fabric or toile de Jouy; these fabrics, which can be glimpsed through the holes in the broderie anglaise, provide a backing that prevents the lavender from falling out of the bag.

Patchwork Lavender Bag with Candy Stripes

You will need

- 5 x 3 inches broderie anglaise
- 5 x 3 inches solid-colored fabric to back the broderie anglaise
- 5 x 3 inches striped fabric
- 3-inch square broderie anglaise
- 3-inch square solid-colored fabric to back the broderie anglaise
- 3-inch square striped fabric
- Two 7 x 5-inch pieces lining fabric
- 7 x 5 inches linen for the back of the bag
- Matching sewing thread
- Approx. 20 inches ribbon or cord

Left: The delicacy of broderie anglaise is best appreciated on small-scale objects, such as these lavender bags.

1. Place the broderie anglaise rectangle on top of the solid-colored rectangle. Right sides together and taking a ½-inch seam on the broderie anglaise, stitch the two pieces together. Repeat the process with the square pieces of fabric. Press open the seams.

2. Right sides together, taking a ½-inch seam, machine-stitch the rectangles and squares together to form a long rectangle, and press open the seam so that the piece lies flat.

4. Right sides together, taking a ½-inch seam, machine-stitch one short end of the second piece of lining fabric to one short end of the fabric used for the back of the bag.

5. Right sides together, taking a ½-inch seam, machine-stitch the back of the bag to the front, stitching along the right-hand edge of the front piece.

6. Right sides together, fold the fabric in half widthwise. Insert a pin 1 inch either side of the center seam, and machine-stitch from the top and bottom edges up to these points.

8. Turn the bag right side out, with the lining on the inside. Machine-stitch a line around the top of the bag, 1 inch from the top. This forms a channel for the drawstring.

9. Turn the bag inside out again. Machine-stitch around the base, and trim the corners to reduce the bulk of the fabric.

10. Turn the bag right side out. Attach a safety pin to one end of a length of ribbon or cord, and feed it through the channel at the top of the bag to make a drawstring. Fill the bag with lavender.

3. Right sides together, taking a ½-inch seam, machine-stitch one piece of the lining fabric to the top of the bag.

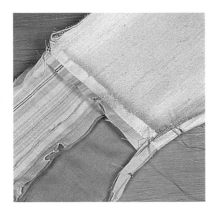

7. Reinforce the points where the machine stitching ends with a few tiny hand stitches. Fold back the raw edge between the pins and slipstitch to secure.

Broderie Anglaise and Toile de Jouy Lavender Bag

You will need

- 10 x 8 inches toile de Jouy
- 10 x 7 inches broderie anglaise
- 10 x 8 inches interlining
- 20 inches narrow ribbon

1. Right sides together, position the broderie anglaise on top of one long edge of the toile de Jouy, overlapping the pieces by about 2 inches. Taking a ½-inch seam, stitch the pieces together. Fold back the broderie anglaise along the stitched line, so that about 1½ inches of the toile de Jouy are visible.

2. Right sides together and taking a ½-inch seam, stitch the interlining to the raw edge of the toile de Jouy.

Above: The soft blue of the toile de Jouy and the subtle green of the broderie anglaise are a beautifully harmonious color combination.

3. Right sides together, fold the piece in half widthwise. Insert a pin ½ inch either side of the center seam, and machine-stitch from the top and bottom edges up to these points.

4. Complete the bag, following Steps 7–10 of the Patchwork Lavender Bag shown opposite.

Laundry Bag

Who says laundry bags have to look boring and functional? This laundry bag is pretty enough to display for all to see and is the perfect way to keep dirty clothes out of sight.

I bought the patterned fabric at an antiques fair and assumed that it was a white linen that had yellowed slightly with age. When I washed it, however, I discovered that the subtle, creamy yellow was actually the original color. I decided to pair it with some pale yellow linen and a soft purple.

The patchwork design comes from a commonly used ceramic tile motif. Patchwork is around us more that we might imagine: look at flooring, church windows, and antique mosaics for inspiration when making up your own designs.

You will need

- Twenty 6-inch squares fabric, some patterned, some solid
- Twelve 2-inch squares purple fabric
- Two pieces lining fabric measuring 26¾ x 20 inches
- 24¾ x 20 inches linen
- Two 48 x 1½-inch strips of purple fabric for drawstrings
- Stiff paper
- Matching sewing thread

Right: The soft colors of the laundry bag fit in perfectly with the pale color scheme of this traditional, country-style bedroom.

1. Using the templates on page 112, cut the backing papers: you will need six A patches, 12 B squares, ten C side patches, and four D corner pieces. Adding ½ inch all around on each piece, cut out the fabric patches. (The B patches should be cut from the purple fabric; the other patches can be made from any toning fabrics.) Baste the fabric patches to the backing papers. Overstitch the six A patches together in three rows of two patches, interspersing them with purple B diamonds.

2. Now fill in the gaps around the edges of the patchwork piece by overstitching the C and D patches that you prepared in Step 1 to make a neat rectangle. The front of the laundry bag is now complete.

3. Fold each strip of drawstring fabric in half lengthwise. Stitch along the length to make a cylinder. Make a strong stitch at one end of the cylinder. Pull the needle and yarn through, pulling the fabric as you go to turn the drawstring right side out.

4. Right sides together and taking a ½-inch seam, machine-stitch one short end of one piece of lining fabric to one short end of the linen that you are using to make the back of the bag. Press the seam toward the lining.

5. Remove the backing papers from the patchwork front of the bag. Right sides together and taking a ½-inch seam, stitch one short end of the other piece of lining fabric to the top of the bag. Press the seam toward the lining.

6. On the sides, about 2½ inches above the seam where the lining fabric is joined to the linen, turn under ½ inch of the lining to the wrong side. Stitching up from the seam, stitch straight for about 2½ inches, and then curve the line of stitching to the edge of the bag. Repeat on the patchwork side.

7. Wrong sides together, fold the lining fabric so that it protrudes about 1 inch above the linen backing fabric: Stitch across the width of the fabric; this forms the channel through which the drawstring will go. Repeat on the patchwork side of the bag.

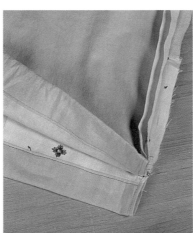

8. Right sides together and taking a ½-inch seam, stitch the patchwork front and its lining to the linen back of the bag and its lining.

9. Trim the corners at the base of the bag to reduce the bulk, and turn the bag right side out. Attach a safety pin to one end of a drawstring, and thread it through the channel at the top of the bag, leaving even amounts protruding. Repeat on the other side.

Clothespin Bag

This pretty little bag is the perfect place to store clothespins and would brighten up any laundry or utility room. It incorporates material from a damaged tablecloth, in which the small, hand-embroidered flowers were spaced so far apart that one could hardly see them. Cutting up the cloth has allowed me to feature them more strongly, so that one can appreciate them properly.

Because I wanted to make a feature of the embroidery, the colors in it dictated the fabrics I used for the rest of the bag. The blue piping highlights the color of the forget-me-not flowers, while the striped orange shirting fabric accentuates the embroidered orange details.

You will need

For the top section of the front of the bag:
- Two pieces of embroidered fabric measuring 10 x 5¼ inches
- Two pieces of striped fabric measuring 10 x 5¼ inches

For the bottom section of the front of the bag:
- Two pieces of embroidered fabric measuring 8¾ x 5¼ inches
- Two pieces of striped fabric measuring 8¾ x 5¼ inches

For the lining:
- Piece of white cotton measuring 18 x 10 inches
- Piece of white cotton measuring 18 x 8¾ inches

For the back of the bag:
- 18-inch square white cotton
- 18-inch square striped fabric

To trim:
- Approx. 2½ yards piping cord covered with blue silk cut on the bias
- 20 inches blue silk cut on the bias, 1 inch wide
- Paper for pattern
- Matching sewing thread
- Coat hanger

Left: Contrast is the key to the success of this design—orange and blue are complementary colors and are virtually guaranteed to look good together, while the busy stripe of the shirting fabric is balanced by the quieter and more subtle pattern of the embroidered cloth.

1. Alternating embroidered and striped fabrics and taking ½-inch seams, piece together the top and lower sections of the front of the bag as shown.

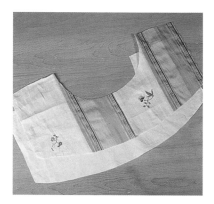

2. Trace the template on page 117 and make a paper pattern for the top section of the front of the bag. Cut one lining piece from white cotton and one from the larger of the two pieced fabrics made in Step 1.

3. Place the top of the bag on top of the cotton lining. Taking a ¼-inch seam, machine-stitch blue silk bias binding around the curve of the top of the bag. Fold the binding over to the back of the bag, turn under ¼ inch, and slipstitch it in place.

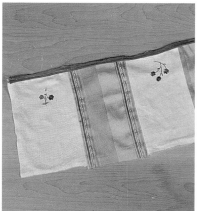

4. Machine-stitch corded piping to the lower section of the clothespin bag, with the raw edges of the binding facing outward.

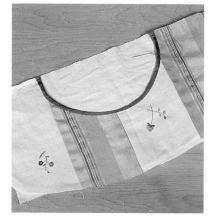

5. Baste the 18 x 8¾-inch piece of white cotton lining to the top of the bag, stitching to the right and left of the curved edge only.

Above: Blue piping around the edge of the bag provides a neat finishing touch and picks up the color of the embroidered flowers.

6. Right sides together, taking a ½ inch seam, stitch the top and lower sections of the bag together, stitching as close to the bias binding as you can.

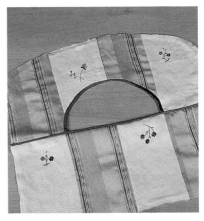

7. Fold down the lining that you attached in Step 5 so that it lies neatly behind the lower section of the clothespin bag.

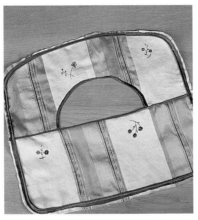

8. Following the instructions on page 124, stitch corded piping around the front of the bag, with the raw edges facing outward.

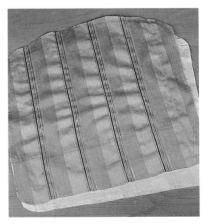

9. Using the pattern on page 116, cut one piece of striped fabric and one piece of white cotton for the back of the bag. Round off the corners.

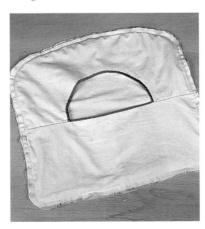

10. Place the back of the bag striped side down with the white cotton lining that you cut in Step 9 on top of it, and the front of the bag striped side down on top of the cotton. Machine-stitch around the edges, leaving a 1-inch gap at the center of the top.

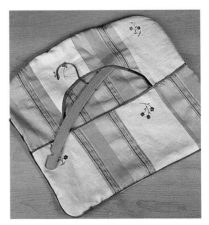

11. Turn the bag right side out, and insert the hook of the coat hanger through the gap at the top. Slipstitch the gap closed to hold the hanger firmly in place.

Vintage-Ribbon Pincushion

The top of this pincushion is based on a traditional Log-Cabin design. What makes this version different—and so easy—is the fact that it is made using ribbons, which don't fray, and therefore you don't have to make seams before adding subsequent layers. The measurements don't have to be exact, either: I've used ribbons of varying widths and textures, which adds to the pincushion's charm.

The yellow ribbon, which has a subtle black line running along the edge, is antique French, while the brown ribbon with the red edge looks as if it could have been used for a military medal ribbon. I combined them with some brightly colored purple and pink ribbons to make the design look more contemporary.

Right: This pretty pincushion, its top made from vintage ribbons, is an eye-catching and practical addition to your sewing kit.

Vintage-Ribbon Pincushion

You will need

- 5-INCH CIRCLE MUSLIN FOR FOUNDATION FABRIC
- SCRAPS OF RIBBON
- 14 X 3 INCHES WHITE LINEN FOR SIDE PANEL
- 5-INCH CIRCLE WHITE LINEN FOR BASE
- ENOUGH CORDED PIPING TO GO AROUND THE TOP AND BASE
- MATCHING SEWING THREAD
- KAPOK OR BATTING FOR FILLING

The finished pincushion measures: approximately 4 x 2 inches.

1. Machine-stitch the first square of fabric, which should measure 2 inches square, to the foundation circle. Machine-stitch one strip of ribbon over each corner of the first square, at right angles to each other so that the center square appears to be set "on point."

2. Machine-stitch a second round of ribbons over the first, again at right angles to each other. In this way, the pattern builds up as a series of concentric wedges. The stitching of the first round of ribbons will be covered up when you add the second round.

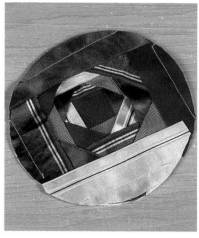

3. Continue until the pieced top is the size you want, and trim the last round of ribbons level with the foundation circle. Here, I attached five "rounds" of ribbons.

4. Following the instructions on page 124, make enough corded piping to go around the top and bottom of the pincushion. With the right side of the top facing upward and the raw edges of the piping facing outward, stitch the piping to the top of the pincushion.

5. Machine-stitch piping to the base of the pincushion in the same way, taking care to make a neat, regular-shaped circle.

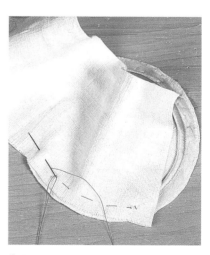

6. Right sides together, baste the side panel to the base, gently easing the fabric around the curve of the base piece.

Above: There's no excuse for losing pins when you have this decorative pincushion to hand! It would make the perfect gift for any enthusiastic needlewoman.

7. Machine-stitch the side panel to the base of the pincushion, stitching as close as possible to the stitched line of the piping and cutting small nicks into the side panel to reduce bulk and ease it more readily around the curve of the base piece.

8. Right sides together, baste the ribbon-patchwork top to the other end of the side panel, clipping the edges as before.

9. Machine-stitch the top to the side panel, leaving the side seam open. Turn the pincushion right side out, and stuff it with kapok or batting. Turn under the raw edges of the side seam to the inside of the pincushion, and slipstitch the gap closed.

Padded Coat Hanger with Heart-Shaped Lavender Bag

Padded coat hangers hark back to a time when garments were hand sewn and made to measure and are a great way of keeping the sleeves of delicate garments in shape. This simple design, with a different fabric on each side and finished off with a strong blue rickrack braid, is crying out for a pretty summer dress to be displayed on it.

The pink silk satin came from a negligée that was falling apart; I combined it with some blue striped fabric that matches the rickrack edging of the hanger.

To keep your garments fragrant, add a little patchwork heart made from two contrasting silks and filled with lavender.

Right: This padded coat hanger, with its heart-shaped decoration, is far too pretty to hide away in a closet. Make it a feature of your bedroom—perhaps displaying a vintage shawl or negligée.

Padded Coat Hanger

You will need

- 20 x 3½ inches white linen
- 20 x 3½ inches silk
- Approx. 45 inches rickrack braid
- Batting
- Matching sewing thread

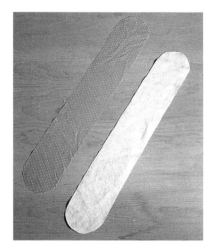

1. Using the template on page 115, cut out one patterned silk and one white linen piece.

2. Machine-stitch rickrack braid in a toning color, or any other decorative trim of your choice, all around the edge of the piece of patterned silk that you cut in Step 1.

3. Right sides together, machine-stitch the linen to the silk, leaving half of one side of the hanger unstitched. Wrap batting around the coat hanger, securing it in place with thread.

4. Turn the coat hanger cover right side out, and place it on the padded hanger. Slipstitch the gap closed, folding under the raw edges of both the linen and the silk.

Heart-Shaped Lavender Bag

You will need

- SCRAPS OF TWO CONTRASTING SILKS— ONE STRIPED, ONE PATTERNED
- 5-INCH SQUARE OF THE SILK USED TO MAKE THE COAT HANGER
- MATCHING SEWING THREAD
- LAVENDER OR ROSE-SCENTED POTPOURRI
- 12-INCH LENGTH OF NARROW SILK OR SATIN RIBBON

I. Cut two 3-inch squares of two contrasting silks, and stitch them together. Press open the seams.

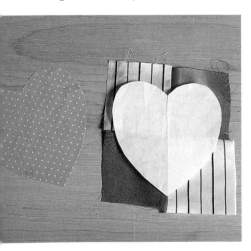

2. Using the template on page 115, make a paper template for the heart. Cut one heart from the patchworked silk and one from the patterned silk used to make the coat hanger cover.

3. Place the two hearts right sides together, and machine-stitch around the edge, leaving a 2-inch gap.

4. Turn the heart right side out, and stuff with lavender or rose-scented potpourri. Fold a length of ribbon in half, place the raw ends in the gap, and slipstitch the gap closed.

Basket Liner

I wanted to make a simple straw basket into something more decorative and decided to add a crisp white linen liner edged with a strip-pieced trim. Inspired by the warm, rich colors of the south of France, I chose fabrics containing red, terra-cotta, and a deep turquoise that reminded me of the sea. I used the same fabrics to make a patch pocket—a handy place to store your shopping list or house and car keys.

You will need

For the liner:

- SCRAPS OF THREE COLORED AND PATTERNED FABRICS FOR THE PIPING AND TIES

- TWO PIECES WHITE SHEETING OR LINEN MEASURING THE CIRCUMFERENCE OF YOUR BASKET BY THE DEPTH OF YOUR BASKET, PLUS $1/2$ INCH ALL AROUND

- ONE PIECE WHITE SHEETING OR LINEN LARGE ENOUGH TO COVER THE BASE OF YOUR BASKET

For the patchwork pocket:

- 3-INCH SQUARES OF EACH OF THE THREE PATCHWORK FABRICS (SIX OF ONE, AND EIGHT OF THE OTHER TWO)

- $8^{1}/_{2}$ x $7^{1}/_{2}$ INCHES WHITE SHEETING OR LINEN FOR POCKET LINING

- MATCHING SEWING THREAD

Right: A crisp white liner, trimmed with bold colors, turns this rustic-looking basket into something altogether more stylish and sophisticated.

1. First make the bias binding. Following the instructions on pages 122–123, cut your three fabrics on the bias into strips that are approximately 3 x 1½ inches and join them together to make one strip that is long enough to go around the top of the basket liner.

2. Make more bias binding for the ties. You will need eight 14½ x 1½-inch strips. Fold each strip in half lengthwise, right sides together, and machine-stitch along the length about ¼ inch from the fold. Turn right side out, and slipstitch the ends closed.

3. Now make the liner. Measure the rim and depth of the basket, and add ½ inch all around. Cut out a piece of sheeting or linen to this measurement, and join the ends together to make a tube.

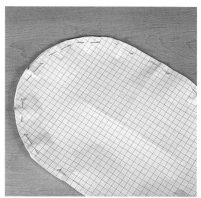

4. Make a paper pattern for the base of your basket, and cut out a piece of sheeting or linen to this measurement, adding ½ inch all around.

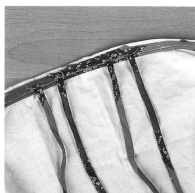

5. Machine-stitch the long strip of bias binding around the liner top with the raw edges facing outward. Stitch one tie on each side of each basket handle.

6. Repeat Step 3 to make a second tube of sheeting or linen. Right sides together, attach it to the first tube, stitching along the line of the bias binding.

7. Right sides together, pin, baste, and machine-stitch the base of the liner to the tube, gathering the tube to get it to fit neatly.

8. Now make the patch pocket. Using the template on page 111, cut 22 backing papers. Adding 1/2 inch all around, cut out eight patches each from two of the patchwork fabrics and six patches from the third fabric. Baste the fabric to the backing papers.

9. Right sides together, oversew along the edges to join the hexagons together in alternating rows of five and six patches. Remove the backing papers and trim to make a rectangle.

10. Now make the lining for the pocket. Right sides together and taking a 1/2-inch seam, machine-stitch one long end of the sheeting or linen lining to one long end of the patchwork.

11. Right sides together, fold the pocket so that the lining protrudes about 3/4 inch above the patchwork. Machine-stitch around the edge, leaving a 3-inch gap in one side for turning.

12. Turn the pocket right side out, and slipstitch the gap closed. Turn the liner right side out, and appliqué the pocket to it.

Table Runner, Place Mat, and Napkin Ring

This coordinating table linen is made out of a beautiful piece of antique patterned linen, whose design has survived very well, combined with modern linen in a strong, dark pink. The bold pattern of the antique fabric and the rich pink of the backing look particularly striking against the dark mahogany dining table.

I feel it's important to get some variety into coordinating sets of household linen like this, and so I reversed the fabrics for the table mats and napkin rings, using the antique linen as the backing and binding. Together they give a festive feel to any meal.

Right: A table runner is a brilliant solution when you want to show off a polished wooden table. The mix of vintage fabrics, bright colors, and simple, unfussy crockery and glassware gives the display a very contemporary feel.

Place Mat

You will need for each place mat:

- 12 x 9 inches solid-colored linen
- 12 x 9 inches heat-resistant batting
- 14 x 11 inches patterned linen
- Chalk powder
- Embroidery floss in a contrasting color
- Quilting needle
- Matching sewing thread

Right: This simple quilted pattern is taken from a linear design that is often used in Japanese prints.

1. Baste the solid-colored linen to the heat-resistant batting.

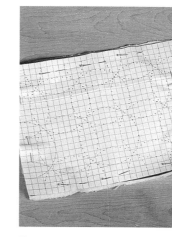

2. Trace the pattern on page 113, or any other decorative design of your choice, onto paper. Prick through the lines of the pattern with a needle to make large holes. Center the pattern on the place mat, and pin in place.

Table Runner

You will need

- 48 x 10½ inches patterned linen
- 48 x 10½ inches heat-resistant batting
- 50 x 12½ inches solid-colored linen
- Matching sewing thread

1. Place the solid-colored linen right side down on a large, flat surface. Center the batting and patterned linen on top, right side up. Fold the solid-colored linen over the patterned linen, and turn under the edge by ½ inch. Pin in place. Slipstitch the edge, and miter the corners.

4. Place the mat in an embroidery frame. Using a quilting needle and embroidery floss in a color of your choice, quilt along the lines of the design, repositioning the hoop as you finish quilting each section of the place mat.

5. Place the patterned linen right side down, and center the mat on top of it. Fold the linen over to the top of the mat, folding under ½ inch so that you get a neat border, and pin in place. Slipstitch, removing pins as you go.

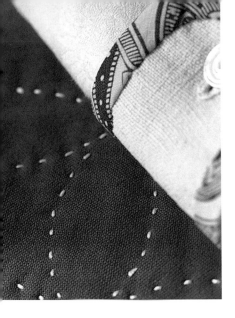

Napkin Ring

You will need for each napkin ring:

- 7½ x 2½ inches white linen
- 7½ x 2½ inches pink linen
- Approx. 22 inches bias binding in patterned linen
- Matching sewing thread
- Button

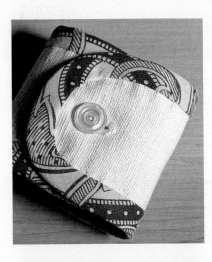

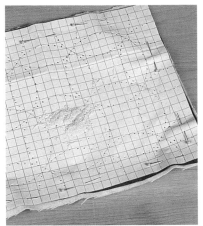

3. Sprinkle chalk powder on top of the pattern, and push it through the holes with your fingers to transfer the pattern to the fabric. You may need to reinforce the lines with a fadeaway pen when you remove the pattern.

1. Using the template on page 113, cut one white and one pink linen piece for each napkin ring.

2. Following the instructions on pages 122–123, make enough patterned linen bias binding to go around the edge of each napkin ring. Place the linen pieces wrong sides together, pin bias binding around the edge, and slipstitch in place.

6. At the corners, fold the backing fabric inward to make a right angle, pressing with your fingers to make a crease. Fold the backing fabric over the corner, and slipstitch in place to make a neat miter.

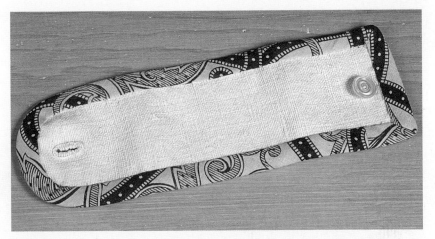

3. Make a buttonhole about 1 inch from one end of the napkin ring. (See page 126.) Stitch a button to the white side of the ring.

Linen Tablecloth with Patchwork Border

The border of this crisp linen tablecloth is made up of a patchwork design fitted into a circle. Although it is shown here on a small occasional table, with its lively, candy-colored fabrics, it would be great for a tea party and could even double up as a picnic rug.

I used the same bold antique floral print in all the large hexagons that run around the border, and selected stripes and solid fabrics in toning colors for the small pieces around each hexagon. This provides continuity throughout the design and also gives the eye a strong pattern on which to focus.

The patchwork border is backed, which gives extra weight to the cloth and allows it to drape elegantly over the edge of a small table.

Right: Although this undulating pattern looks complex, it is, in fact, relatively easy to piece. The key is to think carefully about the positioning of the patterned fabrics so that the design flows harmoniously.

Linen Tablecloth with Patchwork Border

You will need

- APPROX. 2 YARDS WHITE SHEETING AT LEAST 50 INCHES WIDE

- APPROX. 40 x 30 INCHES WHITE LINEN FOR THE BORDER PATCHWORK

- 10 INCHES IN EACH OF SIX 36-INCH WIDE COLORED AND PATTERNED FABRICS FOR THE PATCHWORK

- MATCHING SEWING THREAD

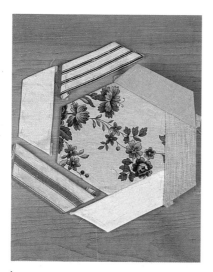

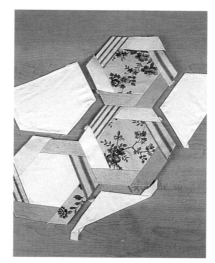

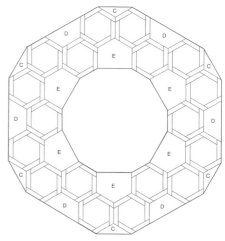

1. Using the templates on pages 118–119, cut 18 backing papers from template A, 108 from template B, and six each from templates C, D, and E. Adding ½ inch all around on each one, cut out the fabric patches. The A and B patches should be cut from an assortment of colored and patterned fabrics, and the C, D, and E patches from white linen. Baste the fabric patches to the backing papers. Right sides together, stitch the B patches around the A patches.

2. Overstitch three of the pieced hexagons together, and add the white linen C, D, and E patches around the edge, as shown above. Make up six blocks of three hexagons in this way.

3. Join the six blocks together as shown above, to make a circular pieced border.

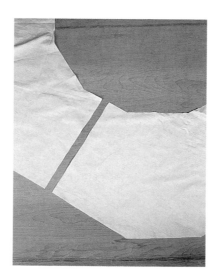

4. Using the pattern on page 119, cut four pieces of white sheeting. Join them together to form the same shape as the patchwork border, taking ½-inch seams. (This is the backing for the patchwork; it adds weight, which helps the cloth to drape well.)

5. Using the pattern on page 119, cut the central portion of the tablecloth from white sheeting.

Right: The striped fabric patches function as arrows, leading the eye through and around the patchwork design.

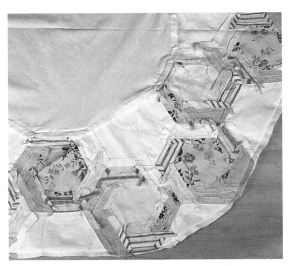

6. Take out the basting stitches, and remove the backing papers from the patchwork border. Right sides together and taking a ½-inch seam, stitch the patchwork border to the white sheeting that forms the central portion of the tablecloth.

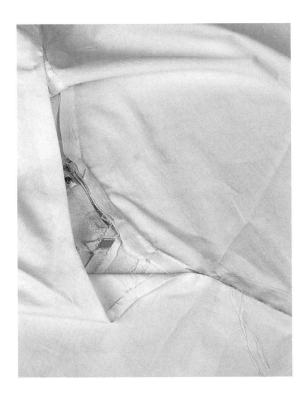

7. Right sides together, stitch around the outside edge of the white sheeting backing and the patchwork border to join them together. Turn the cloth right side out. Fold over the inner edges of the backing by ½ inch, and slipstitch it to the inner portion of the tablecloth, taking care to keep the fabric taut so that it does not wrinkle or pucker.

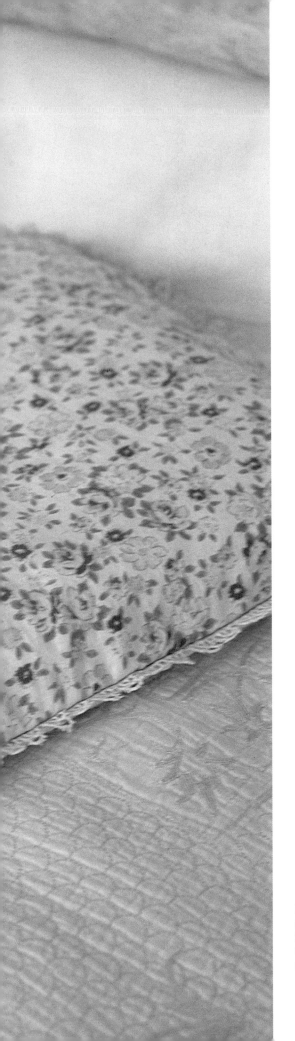

Hot-Water-Bottle Cover

Even in these days of central heating and electric blankets, warming the sheets with a hot-water bottle makes the coldest of winter nights seem bearable.

With a pretty cover made from a feminine-looking floral print combined with a delicate antique lace trim, even something as mundane as a hot-water bottle can be displayed on the end of the bed for all to see. This cover has a padded lining, which makes it soft to the touch and gives some protection from the heat when the bottle is in use.

Left: The soft colors and small-patterned fabric give this hot-water-bottle cover a charming 1930s' feel.

Hot-Water-Bottle Cover

You will need

- 20-INCH SQUARE YELLOW LINEN
- 20-INCH SQUARE LINING FABRIC
- 10 X 6 INCHES GREEN SILK
- 9 X 2 INCHES GREEN SILK
- 9¼ X 9 INCHES FLORAL FABRIC
- 20-INCH SQUARE FOAM OR BATTING
- 9 X 2 INCHES BRODERIE ANGLAISE
- 50 INCHES BRAID OR LACE TRIM

Above: The strip of broderie anglaise in the center of the hot-water-bottle cover adds texture to the piece, as well as providing a visual link with the lace trim around the edge.

Right: Although the fabrics are in soft shades of green and pink, they provide an important touch of color against the white bedspread.

1. Using the top section of the template on page 113, cut out one green silk and one yellow linen piece for the top of the front of the hot-water-bottle cover.

2. Right sides together and taking a ½-inch seam, machine-stitch the two pieces together along the straight edge.

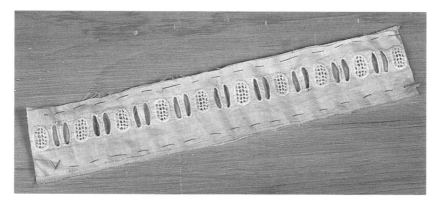

3. Baste the strip of broderie anglaise to the 9 x 2-inch strip of green silk.

4. Right sides together and taking a ½-inch seam, machine-stitch one short end of the floral fabric to one long end of the broderie anglaise. Cut a piece of yellow linen measuring 10¼ x 9 inches. Right sides together and taking a ½-inch seam, machine-stitch the linen to the other side of the broderie anglaise.

5. Trace the template on page 113, and cut a piece of foam or batting ½ inch smaller all around. Place it on the linen portion of the pieced fabric, and fold the broderie anglaise and floral fabric over it to enclose it.

6. Using the template on page 113, cut one linen piece, one lining piece, and one piece of foam or batting that is ½ inch smaller all around. Sandwich the pieces together, with the foam or batting in the middle.

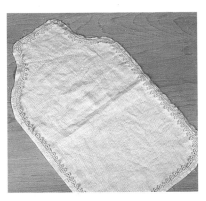

7. Machine-stitch lace trim or a decorative trim of your choice all around the edge.

8. Fold the top piece made in Steps 1 and 2 in half along the seam, and baste it to the back of the patchwork, overlapping it on the patchwork by 1 inch.

9. Right sides together and taking a ½-inch seam, machine-stitch the back to the front, following the stitching line of the lace or decorative trim. Turn right side out.

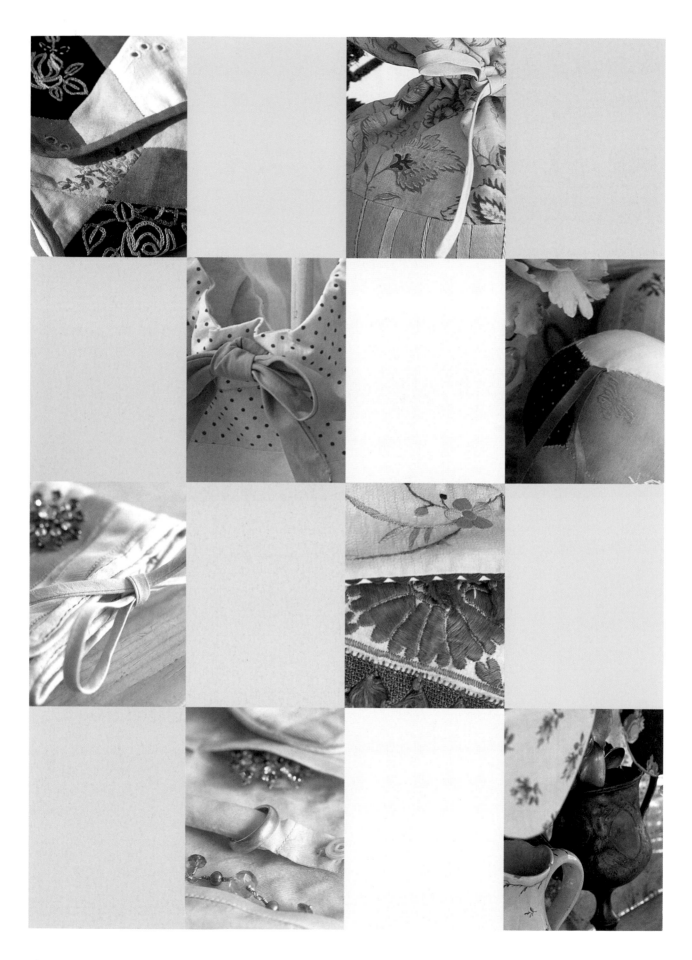

CHAPTER 3

GIFTS AND DECORATIONS

Silk-and-Organza Potpourri Bag

This is a good way of using up a beautiful piece of fabric that is too small to make into anything else. Here, I used a piece of oriental embroidery to make a mitered border for the bag. Although each side is differently patterned, the rickrack edging highlights one of the colors in the embroidery and helps to unify the piece.

The potpourri can be seen through the organza, and the loose weave of the fabric allows the perfume to waft through into the room.

You will need

- FOUR 9 X 3-INCH STRIPS OF SILK
- 8-INCH SQUARE OF ORGANZA
- APPROX. 3 FEET RICKRACK BRAID
- 8-INCH SQUARE OF WHITE LINEN
- MATCHING SEWING THREAD
- POTPOURRI

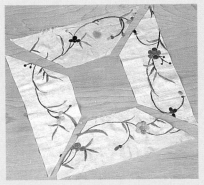

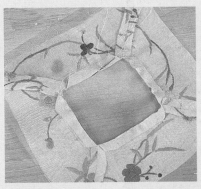

1. Cut each end of each strip of silk at an angle of 45° to make a mitered "frame."

2. Machine-stitch the four pieces of the "frame" together, stopping ½ inch short of the inner edge. Fold the inner edges over to the wrong side, and press with your fingers to hold them in place.

3. Baste and then slipstitch the organza square around the inner edge of the back of the frame, taking care to keep it taut.

4. Machine-stitch rickrack braid in a toning color around the front of the frame, curving the braid around the corners and stitching through the organza, too, to hold it in place.

5. Cut a square of white linen the same size as the frame. Right sides together, stitch the linen to the frame, following the stitching line on the rickrack braid and leaving a 2-inch gap. Round off the corners.

6. Turn the bag right side out, and fill with potpourri in a fragrance of your choice. Slipstitch the gap closed.

Drawstring Cosmetic Bag

Looking around markets and antiques fairs, I came across two fabrics that I thought went well together—a very old floral fabric and an unusual shirting fabric. This cosmetic bag brings the two together. Some light turquoise piping at the base makes the fabrics look fresher and brightens the overall look. A waterproof fabric lining makes the bag practical to use.

Left: No matter how delicate it looks, old linen, which has been laundered for decades, can be revised to make surprisingly sturdy pieces.

Right: Ideal as storage for make-up and bath products, the wash bag has a practical but pretty drawstring, and its artificial silk lining has the advantage of being water resistant.

Drawstring Cosmetic Bag

You will need

- 23 x 7½ inches linen printed with a floral pattern
- 23 x 5½ inches striped fabric
- 23 x 12 inches raw silk for interlining
- 23 x 8 inches synthetic waterproof silk for lining
- 6½-inch square floral fabric for base
- 6½-inch square raw silk for base
- 26 x 1½ inches raw silk for the drawstring
- Approx. 24 inches corded piping
- Matching sewing thread
- Embroidery floss in a toning color

1. Right sides together and taking a ½-inch seam, stitch one long side of the floral fabric to one long side of the striped fabric.

2. Right sides together and taking a ½-inch seam, stitch one long side of the raw silk interlining to one long side of the waterproof silk, 4½ inches from the top.

3. Right sides together and taking a ½-inch seam, stitch the raw silk to the floral fabric to make a long rectangle. (The silk will be folded down inside the bag to form the lining in the final stages.)

4. Fold the rectangle in half widthwise, right sides together. Taking a ½-inch seam, machine-stitch along the long raw edge to make a cylinder.

5. Following the instructions on page 124, cut strips of raw silk in a contrasting color on the bias and make enough corded piping to go all around the base piece. Place the floral fabric base right side up on top of the raw silk base. Place the piping around the edge of the base pieces, with the raw edges facing outward, and machine-stitch in place, stitching ½ inch from the edge and gently curving the piping around the corners.

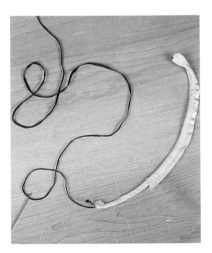

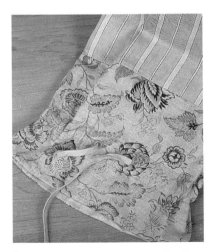

6. Fold the silk lining back over the floral and striped fabrics. Place the base piece, with the piping attached, right side up. Pin the raw edges of one end of the cylinder to the base so that the cylinder fits just outside the square of piping, and stitch it in place, stitching as close as possible to the stitching line of the piping cord.

7. Fold the raw silk for the drawstring in half lengthwise, right sides together, and stitch along the length about ³⁄₈ inch from the fold to make a cylinder. Trim the raw edges. Thread a darning needle with ribbon or embroidery floss, and make a strong stitch at one end of the cylinder. Pull the ribbon through the cylinder, pulling the fabric as you go to turn the drawstring right side out. Tuck in the raw edges, and slipstitch the cylinder closed.

8. Turn the bag right side out. Stitch two parallel lines 2 inches and 3 inches from the top of the bag. Cutting through the floral fabric only, make two small holes about 1 inch apart between the rows of stitching. Work buttonhole stitches around the edges to prevent fraying. Attach a small safety pin to one end of the drawstring, and feed it through the channel, leaving an even length of drawstring protruding from each hole.

Jewelry Roll

This jewelry roll, with its internal compartments and ring holder, is the perfect way to transport your precious trinkets and gems when you go on vacation. The exterior is made from an old piece of Victorian skirt fabric, made colorful and eye-catching with the addition of military ribbons. The ribbons are not applied symmetrically, but this only adds to the overall charm.

Left: With its opulent silk lining and trim, the jewelry roll is a stylish and luxurious-looking addition to any dressing table.

Above left: Cream silk ties keep the roll neatly closed.

Above right: Brooches and bracelets can be tucked away in the internal compartments and rings slotted onto the padded ring holder, with its attractive button fastening.

You will need

- 16 x 9 inches striped fabric
- Approx. 20 x 24 inches cream silk
- 12-inch square of turquoise silk
- Five 16-inch lengths of $1/2$-inch ribbons in five toning colors of your choice
- Enough corded piping to go around the top of the roll
- Matching sewing thread
- Kapok or batting

1. Machine-stitch lengths of ribbon in toning colors to the top of the striped fabric, following the direction of the stripes. Don't worry too much about spacing them evenly, as a little irregularity in the design only adds to its charm.

2. Following the instructions on page 124, make enough corded piping to go around the top of the jewelry roll. With the right side of the jewelry roll facing upward and the raw edges of the piping facing outward, stitch on the piping. Round off the corners.

3. Now make the bottom of the small pocket. Cut a piece of cream silk measuring 12 x 9 inches and a piece of turquoise silk measuring 9 x 5 inches. Right sides together and taking a 1/2-inch seam, stitch the turquoise silk to one short end of the cream silk.

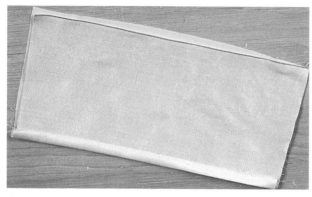

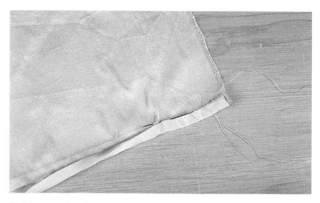

4. Now make the top of the small pocket. Cut a piece of cream silk measuring 9 x 4½ inches and a piece of turquoise silk measuring 9 x 5½ inches. Taking a ½-inch seam, stitch the two pieces together. Fold the top of the pocket so that ½ inch of the turquoise fabric protrudes above the seam.

5. Now make the big pocket. Cut a piece of cream silk measuring 9 x 8 inches and a strip of turquoise silk measuring 9 x 2 inches. Right sides together and taking a ½-inch seam, stitch one long edge of the turquoise strip to one long end of the cream silk. Fold the turquoise fabric over to the back of the pocket, turn under about ½ inch along the raw edge, and handstitch it to the back of the pocket with tiny slipstitches.

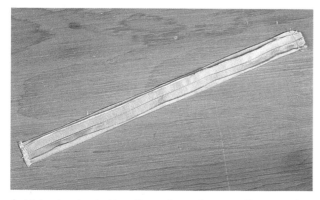

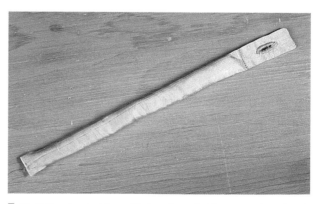

6. Make the ring holder. Cut a piece of cream silk measuring 8 x 2½ inches, fold it in half lengthwise, and stitch along the long edge and one short edge to form a tube. Turn the tube right side out and press it with a warm iron so that the seam lies at the center.

7. Stuff the ring holder with kapok or batting, stopping about 1½ inches before the end. Machine-stitch across the ring holder at this point. Turn under the raw edge, and slipstitch it closed. Make a buttonhole in the center of the unstuffed portion of the ring holder. (See page 126.)

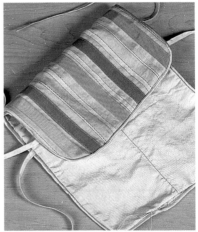

8. Assemble the inside of the roll. Place the large pocket right side up at one end of the interlining and the top of the small pocket right side up on top of the turquoise fabric that has been stitched to the other end of the interlining.

9. Place the ring holder in the center of the roll, with the buttonhole end about ½ inch inside the edge of the interlining. Make four 15-inch cream silk ties, and position them as shown. Baste the pieces together, and machine-stitch a line across the center of the large pocket to divide it into two sections.

10. Place the inside of the roll right side up with the outside of the roll right (striped) side down on top of it. Stitch around the edge to join all the pieces together, stitching as close to the line of the piping as possible and leaving a gap of about 3 inches for turning. Turn the roll right side out, and slipstitch the gap closed.

Day Bag

With its small polka dots, the pink and light green color scheme, and the bows of the handles, this delightful little day bag has a lovely 1950s' feel to it. Over the years, the sun has faded the floral pattern, leaving just parts of the design. This is quite common in antique fabrics, and some designers make it a feature of their creations.

The bag itself is the perfect size for a paperback book, a pair of sunglasses, and a tube of sun-tan lotion—all a girl needs to chill out on the beach or in the park!

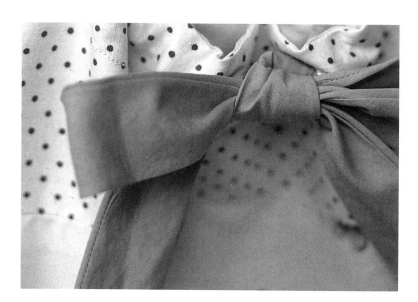

Right: Made from crisp cottons, this delightful little bag can be folded away when not in use, making it the perfect choice to pack in your vacation suitcase.

Day Bag

You will need

- 25 x 12½ inches polka dot fabric
- Two pieces of floral fabric, each measuring 12½ x 5¼ inches
- Two pieces of green lining fabric, each measuring 14 x 13 inches
- two 40 x 3-inch strips pink fabric for the handles
- Matching sewing thread

1. Using the template on page 116, cut out pieces of polka dot fabric for the top section of the front and back of the bag. Cut two floral and two polka dot pieces measuring 12½ x 5¼ inches, and arrange them as shown.

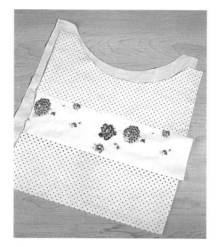

2. Right sides together and taking ½-inch seams, machine-stitch the pieces together as shown. Repeat for the back of the bag. Using the template on page 117, cut out two pale-green cotton lining pieces. (Dye white sheeting if you cannot find exactly the right shade.)

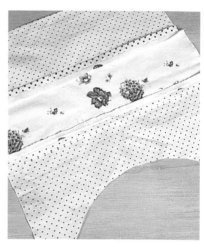

3. On the front and back pieces and the two lining pieces, turn over the top edge of the handle by ½ inch and machine-stitch.

5. Right sides together and taking a ½-inch seam, machine-stitch the front to the back, stitching around the center and bottom bands of fabric only. Round off the corners to reduce the bulk of the fabric and give them a neat finish.

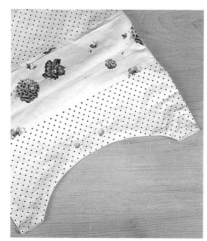

6. Turn the bag right side out. Stitch around the curve of both the back and the front, stitching 1 inch from the edge. Following the instructions on page 126, make two buttonholes in the curved top of the bag, cutting through the polka-dot fabric only.

7. To make the straps for the handles, fold the strips of pink fabric in half lengthwise. Machine-stitch along one short end and the raw edge, stitching about ½ inch from the raw edge. Turn the strip right side out, and slipstitch the open end closed.

Right: A tightly tied bow not only looks attractive, it also provides sturdy handles.

4. Right sides together, stitch the front of the bag to the lining, stitching around the top band of spotted fabric only along the lines marked on the template on page 117. Cut nicks into the curved top edge so that it will lie flat. Repeat the process for the back of the bag.

8. Thread the straps through the channel at the top of the bag from each end and out through the buttonholes, leaving equal amounts protruding from each hole. Tie each strap firmly in a double bow to make a sturdy but decorative handle.

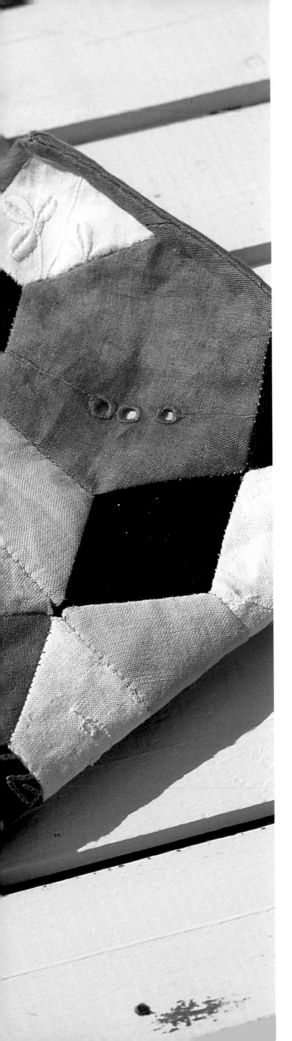

Girl's Patchwork Star Bag

This patchwork bag, ideal for a young girl, is made lively by the use of a variety of stunning pinks and blacks matched with a vivid green silk lining. Although it is unmistakeably vintage, with its delicate floral crewelwork on washed wool, silk, and linen, the contemporary-style geometric pattern and bright colors make it perfect for the most fashion-conscious teenager. The size of the project means that it is ideal for both machine- and hand-piecing.

You will need

- STIFF PAPER
- FABRIC SCRAPS AT LEAST 4 INCHES SQUARE FOR THE PATCHWORK
- APPROX. 20-INCH SQUARE GREEN SILK FOR LINING
- 6-INCH SQUARE WHITE LINEN
- 2½ YARDS BIAS BINDING
- MATCHING SEWING THREAD

Left: Although the fabrics are randomly placed, the jewel-like colors create a wonderfully vibrant effect.

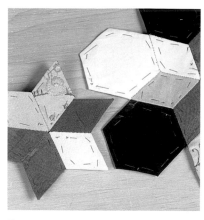

Right: Broderie anglaise and floral motifs embroidered in a flowing chain stitch provide interesting textures. When you're cutting into embroidered fabrics for patchwork, place your template over your chosen motif to make sure you can fit it all in.

1. Using the templates on page 112, cut 44 diamond and 20 hexagon backing papers. Adding ½ inch all around on each piece, cut out the fabric patches. Baste the fabric patches to the backing papers.

2. Right sides together, overstitch diamonds together to make a star. Make four full stars and four half stars. (The remaining diamonds will be used to fill in around the edges of the patchwork.)

3. Assemble the patchwork as shown, interspersing hexagons between the stars. Remove the backing papers, and trim to make a rectangle, allowing ½ inch around the edge.

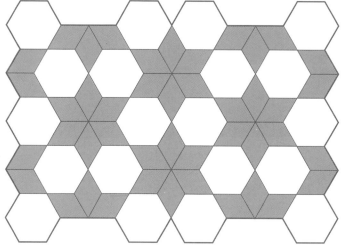

4. Cut a piece of green silk measuring 16½ x 11 inches.

5. Baste the silk to the back of the patchwork and round off the corners on one short edge. (This edge will form the flap of the bag.) Stitch bias binding around the patchwork piece.

6. Using the template on page 112, make two side panels in white linen. Back each one with the same green silk used to line the patchwork. Bind the edge of each side panel.

7. Right sides together, align the unrounded edges of the side panels with the unrounded edge of the main bag and sew them together, following the curved edge of the side panels.

Patched-Pentagon Decoration

These little patchwork decorations are a wonderful way of using up tiny scraps of fabric, as the pentagons used to create them are very small. Some of the fabrics that I used here came from a bag of scraps that I found in an antiques fair; someone had already collected them together and begun making a small patchwork piece. I combined them with silk from men's ties—a great source of colorful and interesting fabrics.

You could hang these decorations from a Christmas tree, display them on a shelf as I have done here, or arrange them in a decorative bowl, perhaps mingled with potpourri, as an attractive table centerpiece.

You will need

- STIFF PAPER FOR BACKING
- SCRAPS OF COTTON AND SILK FABRICS AT LEAST 3½ INCHES SQUARE
- MATCHING SEWING THREAD
- KAPOK OR WOOL FOR STUFFING
- 6 INCHES NARROW RIBBON

1. Using the template on page 111, make 12 backing papers for each decoration. Cut out the fabric patches, adding ½ inch all around each piece. Baste each patch to a backing paper.

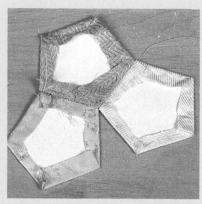

2. Right sides together, overstitch one edge of each pentagon to one side of the central pentagon.

3. Join the two sets of six pentagons together as shown.

4. Continue overstitching the edges of adjacent pentagons together until you have almost completed the sphere, leaving a gap to turn the decoration right side out.

5. Remove the backing papers. Turn the decoration right side out, and fill it with kapok or wool, packing it in tightly so that the decoration is firm to the touch.

6. Fold the ribbon in half lengthwise and insert the cut ends into the gap. Slipstitch the gap closed so that the ribbon loop is firmly secured in place.

Garland

Made from scraps of pretty floral and striped fabrics in contrasting colors, this scallop-shaped garland is a quick-and-easy way of brightening up the edge of a dull shelf.

Try different colorways for different locations and occasions: in festive-looking reds and golds, the same design would make an eye-catching Christmas garland for a banister or mantel shelf, while vibrant primary colors, perhaps stretched across a lawn from tree to tree, would make a jazzy addition to an outdoor party.

You will need

- 6½-INCH SQUARES OF FLORAL AND STRIPED FABRICS IN TONING COLORS
- BIAS CORD APPROX. 10 INCHES LONGER THAN THE TOTAL LENGTH OF THE GARLAND
- MATCHING SEWING THREAD

1. Using the template on page 117, cut two pieces in contrasting fabrics for each "scallop" of the garland. I used a combination of stripes and floral prints, but you could incorporate bold, solid colors if you wish.

2. Right sides together, stitch around the edges, leaving a gap of about ½ inch just below the straight edge on one side and a gap of about 1½ inches on the other for turning. Cut notches around the curve to reduce the bulk of the fabric.

3. Turn the scallops right side out, and slipstitch the larger gap for about 1 inch, until it is about ½ inch in length—just big enough to slip through the hanging cord.

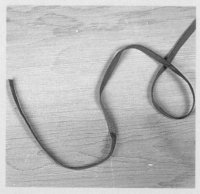

4. For the cord, cut a strip of fabric to the required length, fold it in half lengthwise, and machine-stitch along the length. Turn right side out.

5. Thread the cord through the gaps at the tops of the scallops, and tie a knot in each end to secure it.

Right: Soft prints and stripes tone in beautifully with the stripped wooden shelves in this country-style kitchen.

CHAPTER 4

QUILTS AND THROWS

Linen-and-Damask Crib Quilt

Apart from the backing fabric (a small-scale 1950s' print, which you can just glimpse around the edges), every part of this charming little patchwork crib quilt is white. However, the backing fabric itself is so pretty that you can ring the changes by turning the quilt over and displaying it backing side up.

Much of the white fabric that I used for the top of the quilt is antique damask linen, which often has very beautiful and complex patterns woven into the structure of the cloth. Interspersing squares of this linen with plain, untextured cottons and evenweave linens brings the subtle patterns to life.

Right: Soft and delicate, this delightful quilt would grace any newborn babe's crib.

Linen-and-Damask Crib Quilt

You will need

- THIRTY 5-INCH SQUARES OF WHITE LINEN AND DAMASK
- 21 x 25 INCHES LIGHTWEIGHT BATTING
- 23 x 27 INCHES PRINTED COTTON FOR BACKING
- MATCHING SEWING THREAD

The finished quilt measures: APPROXIMATELY 21 x 25 INCHES.

1. Cut thirty 5-inch squares of white linen and damask. Lay them out on a flat surface and move them around until you are happy with the arrangement. Right sides together and taking ½-inch seams, begin machine-stitching squares together in rows of five, pressing open the seams.

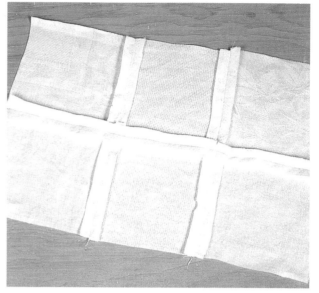

2. Make six rows of five squares. Right sides together and taking care to align the seams neatly from one row to the next, machine-stitch the rows together to complete the top of the quilt—again taking ½-inch seams. Press open the seams so that the piece lies flat.

3. Cut the batting to the same size as the pieced top and the backing fabric 1 inch larger all around. Place the backing right side down on a large, flat surface, and center the batting and pieced top, right side up, on top of it. Working from the center outward, pin or baste the quilt to hold the three layers together.

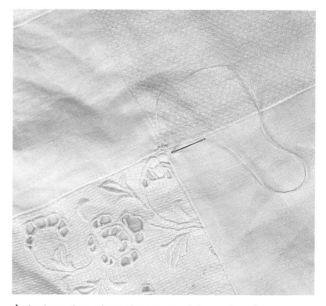

4. At the points where the squares join, make a few tiny stitches through all three layers to secure them, using strong white thread. The stitches will be almost invisible against the white fabric, but it is important to do this in order to prevent the layers of the quilt from slipping around. Remove the pins or basting stitches.

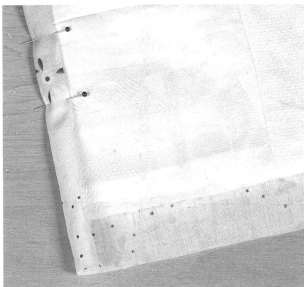

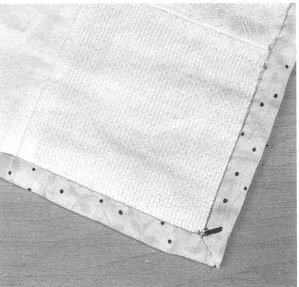

5. Fold the backing fabric over the batting and the quilt top, and fold under ½ inch so that you get a neat, even border all the way around. Pin in place, pinning through all three layers to hold securely. Slipstitch the backing to the quilt top, making your stitches small and as nearly invisible as possible and removing the pins as you go.

6. When you reach a corner, fold the backing fabric over the corner to make a right angle, and crease it with your fingers. Fold the backing fabric from the side of the quilt over the corner to make a neat miter, and slipstitch it in place. The patterned border adds a pretty touch of color to the otherwise all-white quilt.

Summer Quilt in Pink and White

Created from a range of pure vintage cotton fabrics that have all been used in years gone by as children's party dresses, pajamas, old bed linen, and even a favorite summer skirt, this beautiful quilt is the perfect way to make your family memories endure. These much-loved items have been worn to pieces, but it is the fragments, with faded colors and a cozy texture, that create this beautiful quilt. The simple pattern allows you to use your own creativity to create a unique family piece.

Right: Although the quilt is made from fabrics in very subtle, contrasting colors, the star motif is clearly visible.

Summer Quilt in Pink and White

You will need

- STIFF PAPER FOR BACKING PAPER
- 50 INCHES PINK-PATTERNED COTTON 36 INCHES WIDE
- 50 INCHES BLUE-PATTERNED COTTON 36 INCHES WIDE

- APPROX. 100 INCHES WHITE SHEETING, 60 INCHES WIDE
- APPROX. 78 X 53 INCHES PALE PINK FABRIC FOR BACKING
- MATCHING SEWING THREAD
- QUILTING FRAME

- QUILTING NEEDLE
- WHITE QUILTING THREAD
- APPROX. 76 X 51 INCHES BATTING

The finished quilt measures:
APPROXIMATELY 76 X 51 INCHES

1. Using the templates on pages 114–115, cut the following backing papers: 96 A triangles, 24 B squares, 15 C squares (enlarging template by 150 per cent),16 D triangles, and 4 E triangles. Adding ½ inch all around on each piece, cut out the fabric patches; cut equal numbers of two differently patterned A triangles, and all others from white sheeting. Baste the fabric patches to the backing papers. Right sides together, overstitch two pale pink and two blue triangles to each B square.

2. Make 24 pieced units in this way, making sure that matching fabrics are adjacent to one another, as this is how you create the subtle star pattern that is repeated at regular intervals across the quilt top.

4. Turn the pieced top through 45° so that the squares appear to be set on point. Fill in the gaps around the edges with the D triangles, and insert an E triangle at each corner to complete the rectangular shape of the quilt.

5. Remove the backing papers. Assemble the quilt layers, pin, and baste. Using a quilting frame, hand-quilt each white square diagonally from corner to corner. (See page 122 for instructions on how to mark straight quilting lines.)

Right: The quilting—simple white stitches that run diagonally across each white square—is subtle but effective and holds the layers of the quilt together.

3. Assemble the patchwork top in rows, as shown, alternating pieced and plain squares. Overstitch the rows together.

6. Fold the backing over to the front of the quilt, and turn under the fabric by ½ inch to give an even border all the way around. Pin in place. Slipstitch the edge, and miter the corners, removing the pins as you go.

Button Quilt

This quilt was inspired by abstract painters such as Paul Klee, who used simple squares of different colors to create harmonious compositions and moods. The squares of vintage rose-patterned fabric and lavender shirting dictated the colors used in the rest of the quilt. Shirting is a hard-wearing fabric; as men's shirts tend to wear only at the collar and cuffs, re-using this fine, soft weave is both economical and stylish. The buttons on each corner, which provide tiny highlights of color, also hold the fabric layers together—and so the structure of the quilt becomes an integral part of its design.

Right: Although the buttons are brightly colored, they are all relatively dark in tone; the dark edging of the quilt provides a visual link to the buttons and helps to hold the whole piece together.

Button Quilt

You will need

- ONE HUNDRED AND TWENTY 6-INCH SQUARES IN ASSORTED COLORS, SOME PATTERNED, SOME SOLID
- 51 x 61 INCHES BATTING
- 53 x 63 INCHES BACKING FABRIC
- 99 SMALL BUTTONS IN ASSORTED COLORS
- MATCHING SEWING THREAD

The finished quilt measures: 51 x 61 INCHES

1. Lay out the squares in 12 rows of ten squares each on a large, flat surface, and move them around until you're happy with the arrangement; make sure that the patterned fabrics are evenly distributed and that you don't get two squares of the same solid color next to one another. Stitch the squares together in rows, taking ½-inch seams. Press the seams open.

2. Stitch the 12 rows together in the same way, again taking a ½-inch seam allowance and taking care to align the seams from one row to the next. Press the seams open.

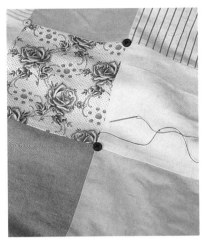

3. Lay the backing fabric right side down on a large, flat surface and smooth out any wrinkles. Center the batting on top, and place the pieced quilt top, right side up, on top of the batting. Working from the center of the quilt outward, pin or baste the layers of the quilt together to prevent them from slipping. Again working from the center outward and stitching through all three layers, stitch a small button at each corner of each square.

4. At each corner, fold the backing fabric inward to make a right angle, pressing the fabric with your fingers to make a crease.

5. Fold the backing fabric over the batting and the quilt top, and fold under ½ inch so that you get a neat border all the way around. Pin in place.

6. Slipstitch the backing to the quilt top, removing the pins as you go and mitering the corners for a neat, crisp finish.

Dotted Sofa Throw

This design of brightly colored dots on a white background is very fresh and modern and looks stunning casually draped over the back of a sofa or armchair. It would also look fantastic displayed on a plain white wall as a piece of textile art. You can adapt the pattern shown overleaf to make it as large or as small as you wish. For a coordinated look, try making matching scatter cushions, using one block for each cushion.

From a distance, the piece looks deceptively simple; closer inspection reveals that the circles are actually octagons and that the background is pieced from many diamonds of white damask. The patterning of the damask gives the piece texture and visual interest as it catches the light.

Right: Shown here on a white upholstered armchair, this throw would look equally at home in a country cottage or a chic modern apartment.

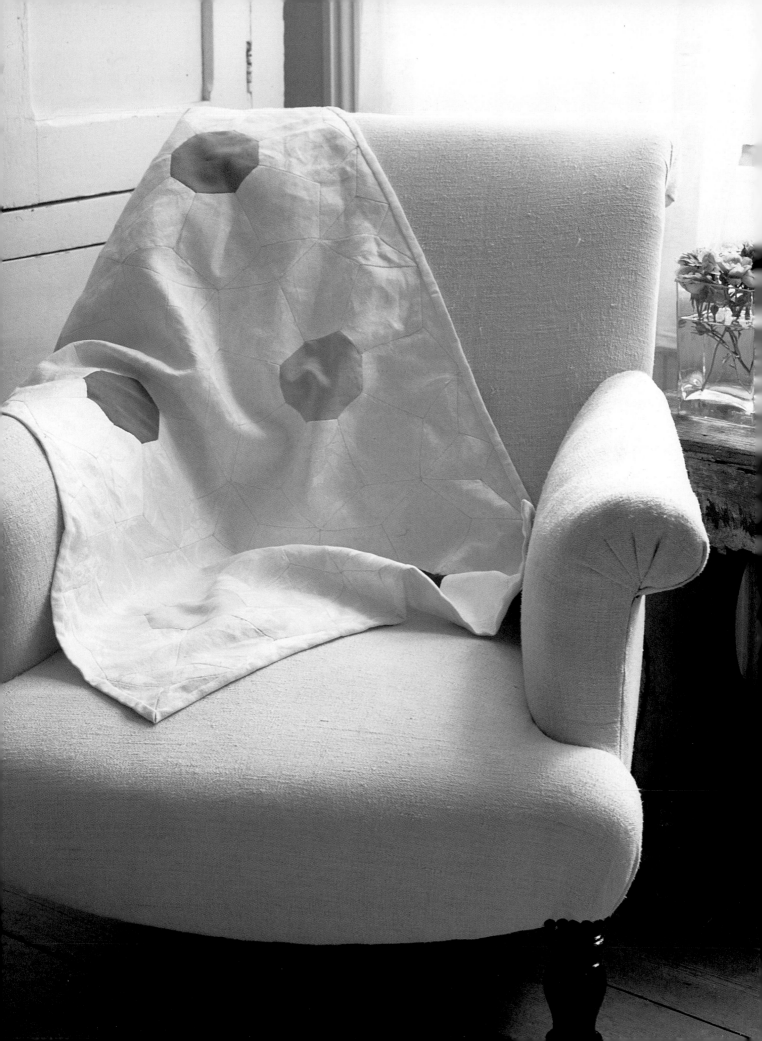

Dotted Sofa Throw

You will need

- SIX 5-INCH SQUARES OF SILK IN DIFFERENT COLORS
- APPROX. 2 YARDS WHITE DAMASK LINEN, 36 INCHES WIDE
- 35 x 25 INCHES PLAIN WHITE LINEN FOR BACKING
- MATCHING SEWING THREAD

1. Using the templates on page 110, cut the backing papers: six octagons (A), 41 thin diamonds (B), 34 large diamonds (C), and 48 pentagons (D). Adding ½ inch all around on each piece, cut out the fabric patches; use colored silks for the octagons and white damask for the other pieces. Baste the patches to the backing papers. Right sides together, overstitch D pentagons around the octagons. Make six blocks, each with a different-colored center.

2. Right sides together, overstitch thin B diamonds around the first of the colored-center blocks. Repeat with the other colored-center blocks so that you have six roughly circular blocks. (Refer to the diagram for Step 4 to see how these six colored-center blocks are joined together.)

3. Make up two blocks of four C diamonds; these will be positioned in the center of the patchwork between the colored-center blocks.

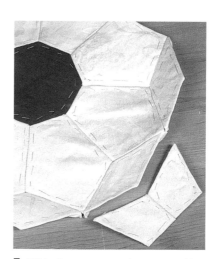

5. To fill in the gaps around the sides of the throw, piece six units of three C diamonds as shown.

6. Attach one of these three-diamond units to the center of each short side and two to each long side (one on either side of the middle colored-center block).

7. Fill in the gaps at each corner with two C diamonds so that you have a neat rectangular shape.

Right: Although it looks, from a distance, as if the colored dots are appliquéd to a white background, the piecing and the use of a textured damask that refracts the light adds visual interest to the piece.

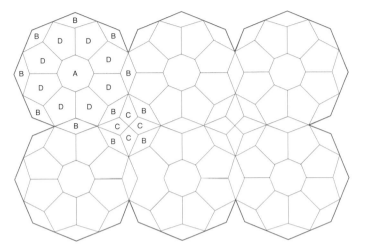

4. Assemble the patchwork as shown. The top of the throw is almost complete; the next stage is to fill in the gaps around the edge to make a neat rectangle.

8. Remove the backing papers, and trim the edges of the patchwork top to make a neat rectangle. Place the backing fabric right side down on a large flat surface, and place the patchwork top, right side up, on top. Pin or baste to hold the two layers together. Fold the backing fabric over to the front, and turn the edge under by 1/2 inch. Slipstitch the edge and miter the corners.

Templates

Dotted lines indicate fold lines

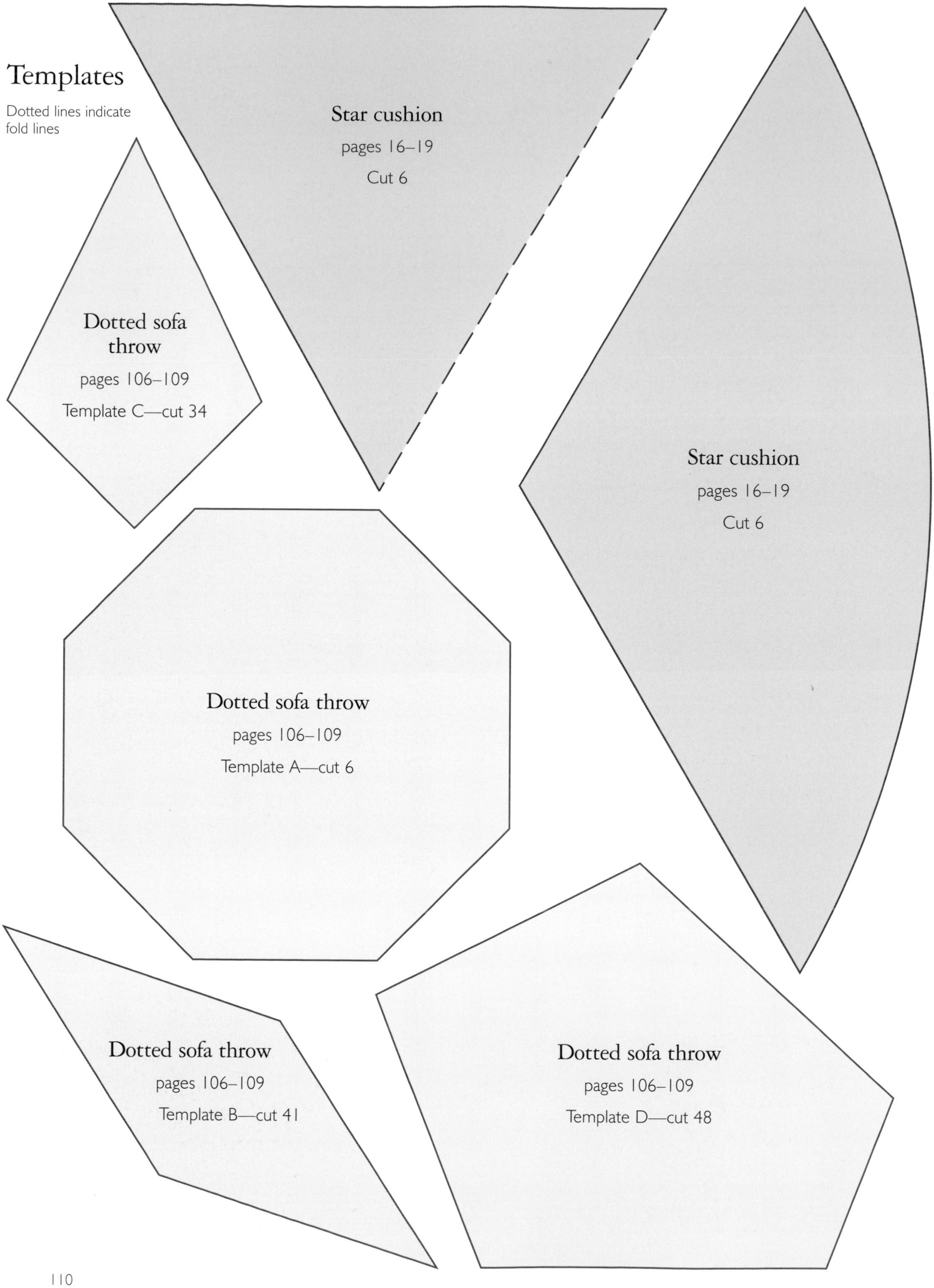

Star cushion

pages 16–19

Cut 6

Star cushion

pages 16–19

Cut 6

Dotted sofa throw

pages 106–109

Template C—cut 34

Dotted sofa throw

pages 106–109

Template A—cut 6

Dotted sofa throw

pages 106–109

Template B—cut 41

Dotted sofa throw

pages 106–109

Template D—cut 48

Tie-on quilted cushion

pages 26–29

Basket liner

pages 52–55

Cut 22

Patched-pentagon
decoration

pages 88–89

Cut 12

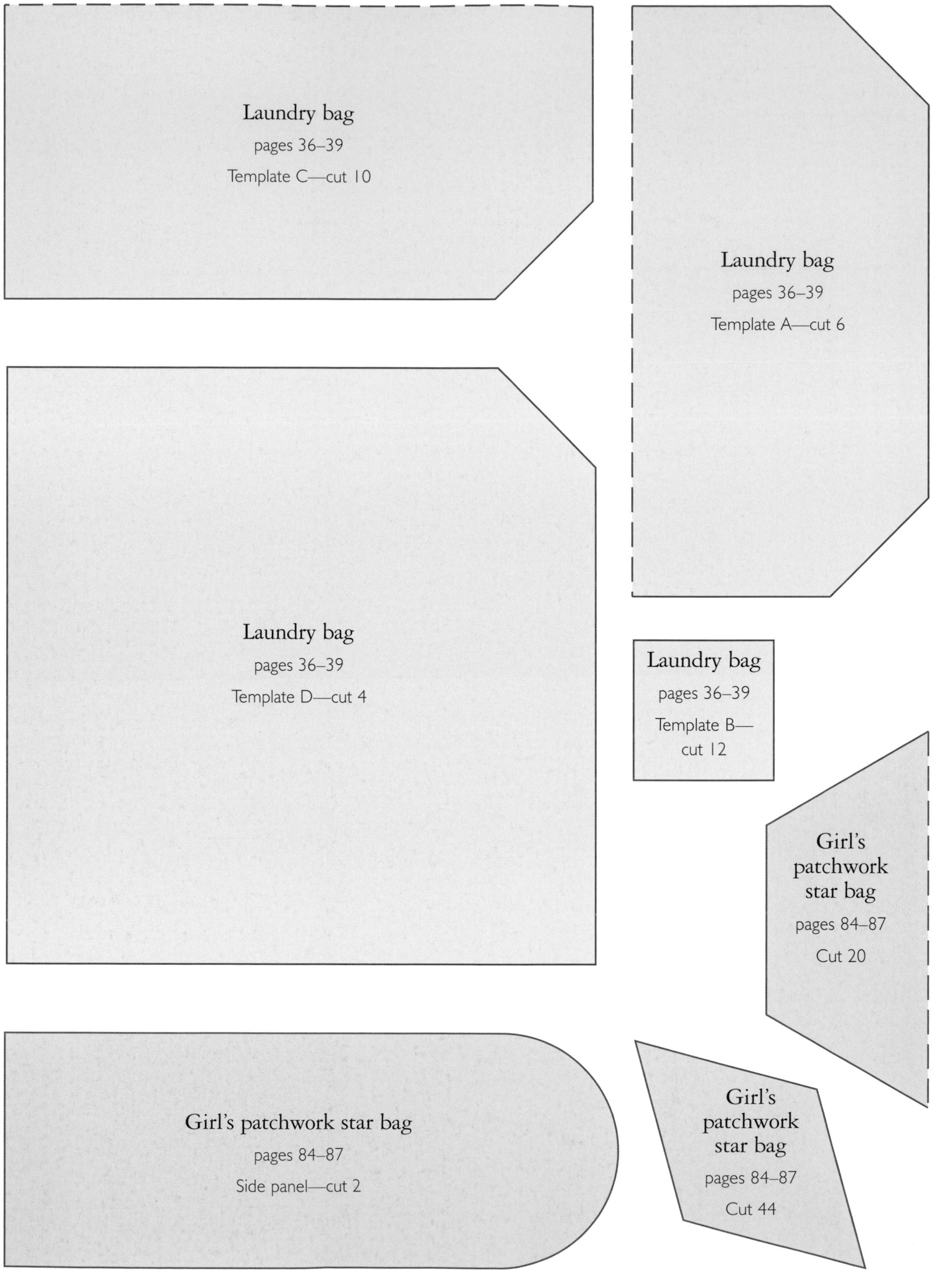

Laundry bag

pages 36–39

Template C—cut 10

Laundry bag

pages 36–39

Template A—cut 6

Laundry bag

pages 36–39

Template D—cut 4

Laundry bag

pages 36–39

Template B—
cut 12

Girl's patchwork star bag

pages 84–87

Cut 20

Girl's patchwork star bag

pages 84–87

Side panel—cut 2

Girl's patchwork star bag

pages 84–87

Cut 44

Napkin ring

page 59

Cut 2

Place mat

(enlarge 200%)

pages 58–59

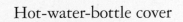

Hot-water-bottle cover

(enlarge 200%)

pages 64–67

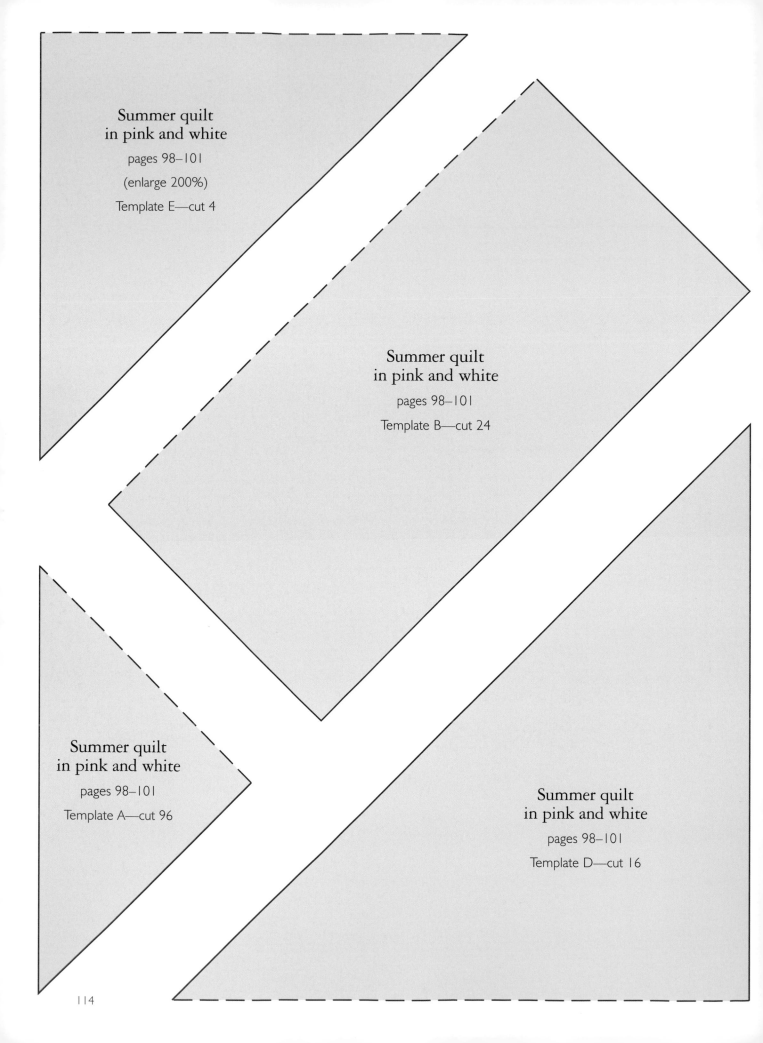

**Summer quilt
in pink and white**

pages 98–101

(enlarge 200%)

Template E—cut 4

**Summer quilt
in pink and white**

pages 98–101

Template B—cut 24

**Summer quilt
in pink and white**

pages 98–101

Template A—cut 96

**Summer quilt
in pink and white**

pages 98–101

Template D—cut 16

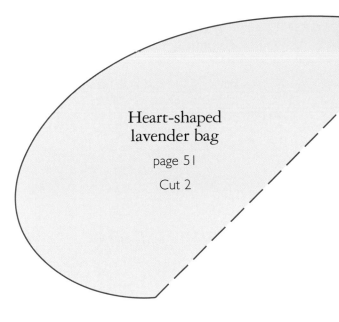

**Heart-shaped
lavender bag**

page 51

Cut 2

Coat hanger

page 50

Cut 2

**Summer quilt
in pink and white**

pages 98–101

(enlarge 150%)

Template C—cut 15

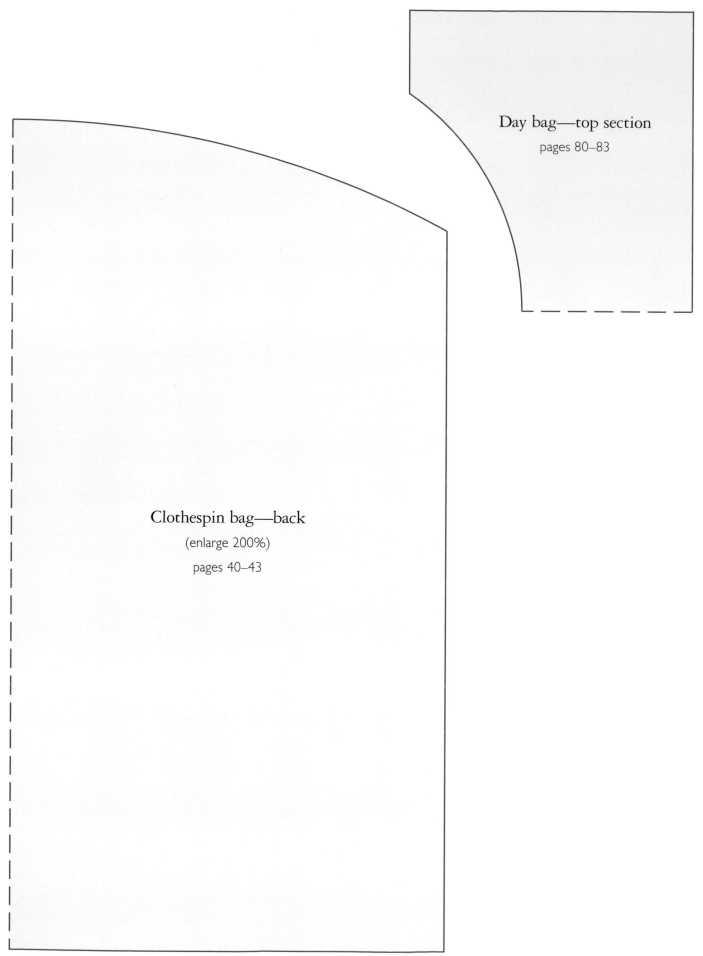

Day bag—top section
pages 80–83

Clothespin bag—back
(enlarge 200%)
pages 40–43

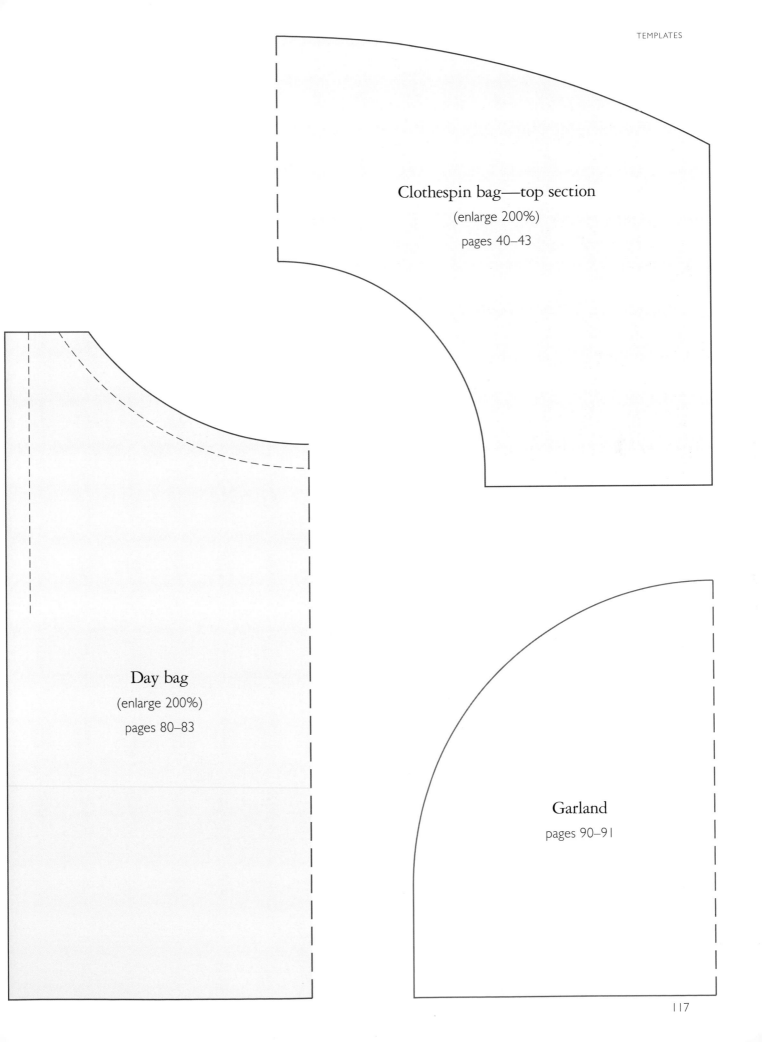

Clothespin bag—top section

(enlarge 200%)

pages 40–43

Day bag

(enlarge 200%)

pages 80–83

Garland

pages 90–91

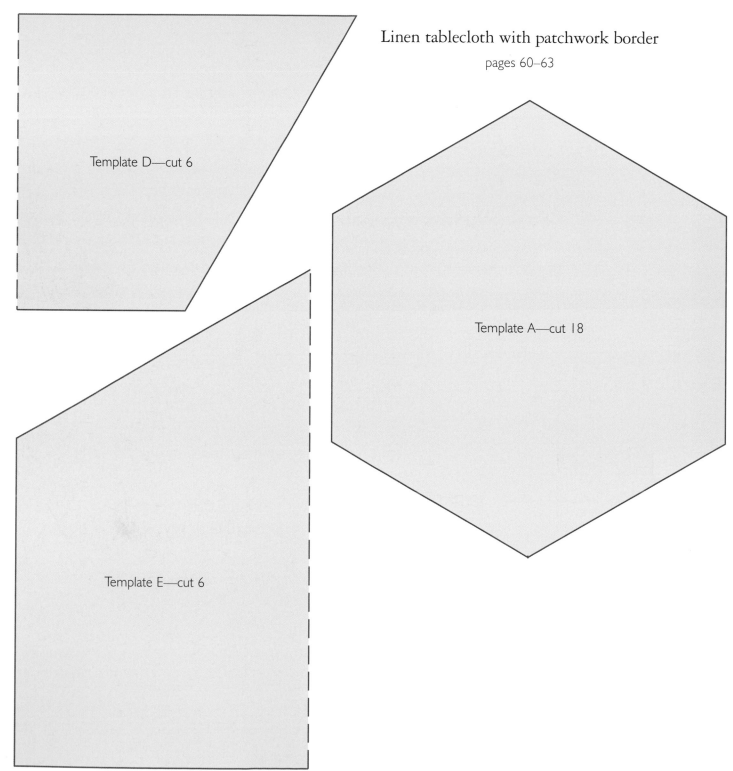

Template C—cut 6

Template D—cut 6

Linen tablecloth with patchwork border
pages 60–63

Template A—cut 18

Template E—cut 6

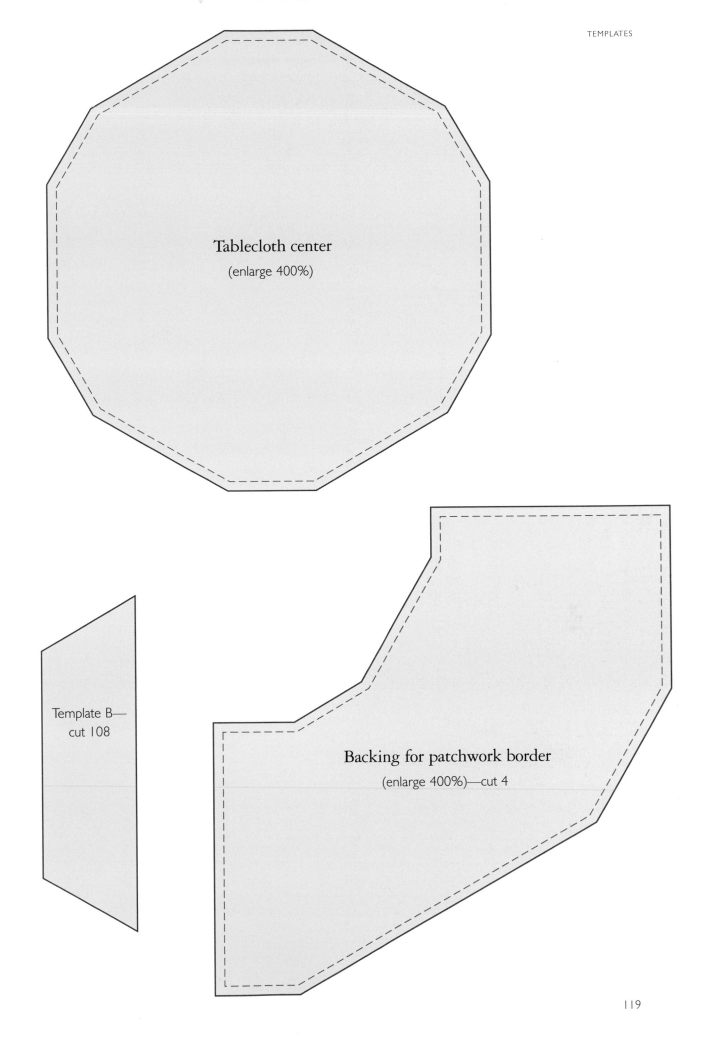

Tablecloth center

(enlarge 400%)

Template B—
cut 108

Backing for patchwork border

(enlarge 400%)—cut 4

TECHNIQUES

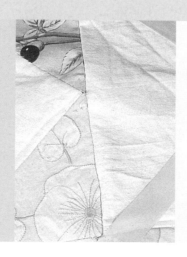
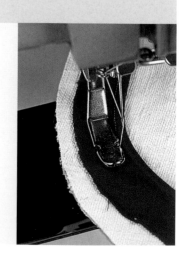

English patchwork

English patchwork is the term given to a method of piecing fabric patches over backing papers. It is used particularly for shapes that have sharp points, such as diamonds and hexagons.

Making a template

1. Trace shapes to the correct size. Using a soft pencil, scribble over the lines to transfer the shape to stiff card. (Alternatively, trace the shape onto template plastic, available from good craft stores.)

2. Place the card on a self-healing cutting mat or on top of several layers of newspaper so that you don't damage your table top. Using a scalpel or sharp craft knife and a metal ruler or straightedge, cut out the template.

Cutting backing papers and fabric patches

Using a sharp pencil, draw around the card template to make the backing papers. You need to use reasonably stiff paper so that it will not bend out of shape, but not paper that is so stiff that it is difficult to stitch through. Place the backing papers on your chosen fabric, aligning the grain if possible, and cut out with fabric scissors, adding ½ inch all around.

Stitching fabric patches

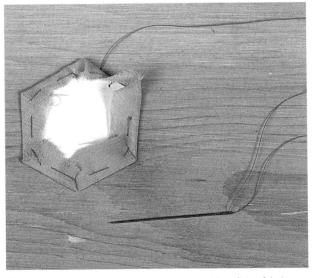

Center the backing paper on the wrong side of the fabric patches. Fold over the excess fabric, making sure that any points are sharp, and baste. Right sides together, overstitch the edges.

121

Marking quilting patterns

Quilting is the term used to describe the process of stitching the three layers of a quilt (top, batting, and backing) together. Before you can begin stitching, you need to mark out where to stitch—and before you can mark the stitch lines, you need to anchor the three layers together so that they do not slip out of

Marking straight lines

The simplest way to mark straight lines is to place low-tack masking tape on the fabric. You can then stitch alongside the tape to get a straight line. However, remember not to leave the tape in position for too long; otherwise, it may mark the fabric.

Marking elaborate patterns

1. Trace your chosen quilting design onto stiff tracing paper. Using a large needle, prick a series of holes along the lines of the quilting pattern.

Hand quilting

If you intend to make lots of full-size quilts, you may find it worthwhile investing in a proper quilting frame; however, they take up a lot of space. A hoop (see below) is a good alternative.

Quilting with a hoop

Place the inner hoop on a flat surface, and center a portion of the item to be quilted over it. Place the outer hoop over the top, and tighten the wing nut to hold the piece taut.

Making bias binding

Making your own bias binding allows you to match the binding to the other fabrics you are using in a particular project.

1. Level the edges of the fabric along the straight grain in both directions. Using a set square and tailor's chalk, mark lines about 1½ inches apart across the fabric at an angle of 45°. Cut out the strips of fabric.

position while you work. Place the backing fabric right side down on a large, flat surface, and smooth out any wrinkles. Center the batting on top, and place the quilt top, right side up, on top of the batting. Working from the center of the piece outward, baste or pin through all three layers.

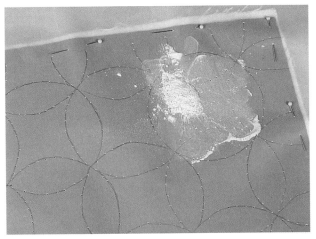

2. Pin the pattern to the item to be quilted. Using your fingers or a soft cloth, rub chalk powder (available from needlecraft and craft stores) though the holes in the pattern to transfer the design to the fabric.

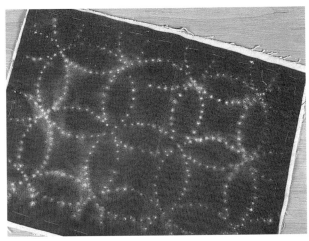

3. Remove the pattern. Go over the lines with a pencil or fabric marker if necessary. (Fadeaway pen is good.) The item is now ready to be quilted.

2. To join strips, place two short edges together along the straight grain and stitch the seam.

3. Press the seam open, and carefully trim away the pointed ends of the seam. Continue adding strips until you reach the required length.

Making corded piping

With corded piping, a length of cord is laid along the center of a strip of bias binding. It has a ridged edge that is particularly effective as an edging for cushions.

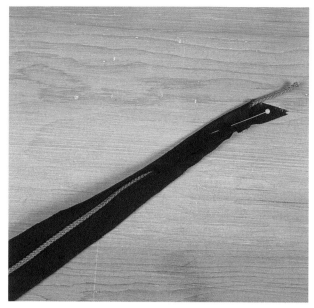

1. Cut a strip of bias binding to the desired length. Fold it lengthwise, wrong sides together, and lay the cord inside the binding along the fold line. Pin through the fabric and the cord at one end to secure.

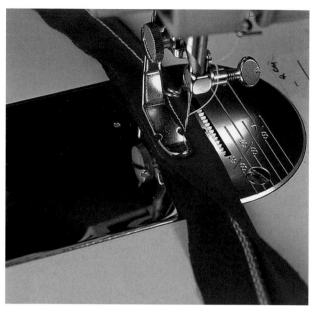

2. Using the zipper foot attachment on the machine, stitch along the edge of but not through the cord.

Attaching piping

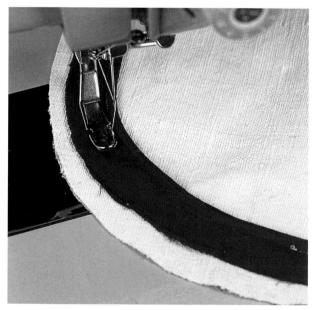

You should always make piping longer than required and trim it when it is in place. Baste the piping to right side of the piece with the raw edges of the piping facing outward. Using the zipper foot attachment, machine-stitch, stitching as close to the piping as possible. When the piece is assembled, the raw edges of the piping will be hidden from view.

Joining corded piping

To join two pieces of cording together (either to make a longer piece or to join two ends of the same piece in a circle), cut the piping so that the two ends of the cord butt together. Wrap thread around the join to bind the two ends together.

Inserting a zipper

A zipper provides a neat, professional-looking way of closing cushions. You must measure and mark the position of the zipper carefully before you stitch it in place.

1. Measure or mark the position for the zipper on the seam, using the zipper as a guide. Stitch the seam up to the markings.

2. Place the closed zipper on the center seam, and pin and baste it in place.

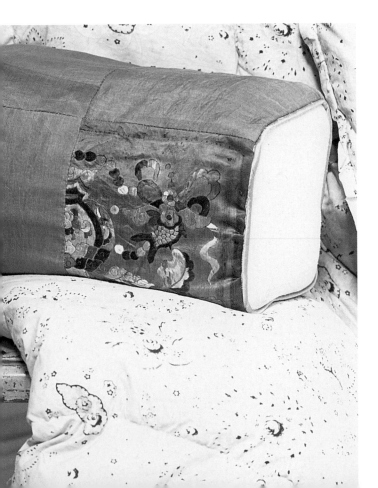

3. Using the zipper foot attachment on the sewing machine, carefully stitch along each side of the zipper and around the closed end.

Making a buttonhole

1. Mark the sides of the buttonhole in pencil, and work small running or back stitches (here shown in a contrasting color of thread for clarity) all around the edge.

2. Using a small pair of sharp scissors, cut a slit in the center of the buttonhole.

3. Work buttonhole stitch around the slit, covering the running or back stitches that you made in Step 1.

Making a pattern for a cushion or chair cover

Although you may be lucky enough to find a cushion pad the right size for your chair, it is worth knowing how to make your own pattern.

1. Take a piece of stiff tracing paper, and place it on the seat of your chair. Measure the front and back edges, and carefully draw a line down the center of the seat. Crease the tracing paper around the edge of the seat.

2. Cut along the crease lines and center line. Place the pattern back on the chair to check that it is symmetrical. Pin the pattern to your chosen fabric, placing the center line on a fold, and cut it out, remembering to add ½ inch all around for the seam allowance.